Essential Histories

The Franco-Prussian War
1870–1871

Essential Histories

The Franco-Prussian War
1870–1871

Stephen Badsey

First published in Great Britain in 2003 by Osprey Publishing,
Midland House, West Way, Botley, Oxford OX2 0PH, UK
443 Park Avenue South, New York, NY 10016, USA
Email: info@ospreypublishing.com

ISBN 978-1-84176-421-4

A CIP catalogue record for this book is available from the British
Library

Typeset in Monotype Gill Sans and ITC Stone Serif

Editor: Sally Rawlings
Design: Ken Vail Graphic Design, Cambridge, UK
Cartography by The Map Studio
Index by Alan Rutter
Picture research by Image Select International
Origination by PPS Grasmere Ltd., Leeds, UK
Printed in China through Bookbuilders

06 07 08 09 10   14 13 12 11 10 9 8 7 6 5

For a complete list of titles available from Osprey Publishing
please contact:

NORTH AMERICA
Osprey Direct, C/o Random House Distribution Center,
400 Hahn Road, Westminster, MD 21157
E-mail: info@ospreydirect.com

ALL OTHER REGIONS
Osprey Direct UK, P.O. Box 140, Wellingborough,
Northants, NN8 2FA, UK
E-mail: info@ospreydirect.co.uk

www.ospreypublishing.com

Dedication

To my parents

Contents

Introduction

The Franco-Prussian War of 1870–71 was the largest and most important war fought in Europe between the age of Napoleon and the First World War. Since it ended in the establishment of a new German Empire, contemporaries often called it the 'Franco-German War', although neither name fits it perfectly. In 1870–71, 'Prussian' forces included those from an alliance of other German states, but Prussia and its interests dominated, just as in the Second World War German armies often included forces from other Axis members. The creation and continued existence of this new united Germany set the agenda for European international politics and war for the next century. The war also marked the end of the French Second Empire under Napoleon III, and with it the end of France's dominant position in Europe. This was something that was never recovered, although in the longer term the war also established France as the most important and enduring republic on the continent. In a wider sense, both sides were conscious of a rivalry for dominance in western Europe between the French and German peoples that went back for centuries, chiefly for control of the lands that lie on either side of the Rhine and its tributaries from the North Sea to the Alps.

Despite its apparently ancient origins, the Franco-Prussian War also marked the beginning of the creation of modern Europe in every sense. It featured a mixture of aristocratic and conservative behaviour based

'Prussian Infantry at the Charge'. Engraving from *The Graphic of London*, 3 September 1870. (Ann Ronan Picture Library)

A DUEL TO THE DEATH.

France: 'Pray stand back Madam. You mean well; but this is an old family quarrel, and we must fight it out!' A cartoon by John Tenniel from the London magazine *Punch*, 23 July 1870. The figure of Britannia (representing Great Britain) attempts to restrain Napoleon III representing France and Wilhelm I representing Prussia. (Ann Ronan Picture Library)

on old ideas of personal rule and the Concert of Europe (see page 13), together with the new realities of power politics and national bureaucracies. It was the first experience of what the Prussians called *Millionenkrieg*, 'the war of the millions', but both sides argued the formalities of international law, and treated the frontiers of neutral countries as if the laws that protected them were unbreakable barriers. Both King Wilhelm I of Prussia and Emperor Napoleon III of France made critical distinctions between their behaviour in the private sphere and as public heads of state. In its conduct also, the war mixed the weapons, tactics and methods of an earlier era with new military science and new political attitudes. Personalities decided this war, but so did armaments factories, public opinion, military staffwork and mass revolution.

The events of the Franco-Prussian War fell into three main phases. Beginning in July 1870, it opened with a short campaign lasting until September, in which the major battles took place, after which it was largely considered to be over. The war continued until January 1871 because both sides could not agree peace terms. Finally, with peace declared and the war officially over, there was an attempted revolution and civil war in Paris known as the Commune. This was suppressed by the French in May, just as the Treaty of Frankfurt formally ending the war came into force.

War was declared by the French over a minor issue, although the circumstances were engineered by the minister-president of Prussia, Count Otto von Bismarck. Prussia was supported by the other members of the North German Confederation, and by the states of southern Germany. Contrary to expectations, it was the Prussians and their allies who invaded France, a move for which the French were unprepared. From this bad start, the French Army suffered a series of humiliating defeats which resulted in one of its two field armies being trapped in Metz, where it surrendered in October after a siege of two months, and the other army being forced to surrender together with Napoleon III himself in early September at Sedan after being defeated and unable to escape.

As a result of these defeats, in September the Second Empire was overthrown in

A French popular print depicting French troops firing on Communards in the Père Lachaise Cemetery and the Chaumont Heights in Paris during the final suppression of the Commune in 'Bloody Week', 21–28 May 1871. (Ann Ronan Picture Library)

Europe at the time of the Franco-Prussian War

1. Prussia and the north German Confederation.
2. Bavaria.
3. Würtemberg.
4. Baden.
5. Territory of Alsace-Lorraine annexed to Germany
    from France in the Treaty of Frankfurt 1871.

0	250 miles
0	500 km

ICELAND
(DENMARK)

ATLANTIC
OCEAN

NORWAY
(SWEDEN)

SWEDEN

St Petersburg

SCOTLAND

NORTH
SEA

DENMARK

BALTIC
SEA

IRELAND

GREAT
BRITAIN

WALES   ENGLAND

London

NETHER-
LANDS

Berlin

①

Brussels

BELGIUM

LUX

Paris

⑤ ④ ③   ②   Vienna

FRANCE

SWITZERLAND

AUSTRO-HUNGARIAN
EMPIRE

Bay of
Biscay

ADRIATIC SEA

ITALY

SERBIA   ROMANIA

PORTUGAL

SPAIN

Corsica

Rome

MONTENEGRO

Black Sea

Balearics

Sardinia

BULGARIA

MEDITERRANEAN

OTTOMAN EMPIRE

Sicily

GREECE

ANATOLIA

MOROCCO

ALGERIA
(FRANCE)

TUNISIA

Malta (GB)

SEA

Crete

France, and the Third Republic established. The Prussians, meanwhile, encircled Paris and started a siege, expecting a quick French surrender. The war then dragged on inconclusively for another four months through the winter of 1870–71, with the Prussians occupying an area of northern France resembling a giant thumb pointing west, with its base on the frontier provinces of Alsace and Lorraine and its tip covering Paris. The new French Third Republic assembled armies to the south, north and south-east with the intention of relieving the siege of Paris. Finally, the miseries of the siege for the people of Paris, the failure of their armies to break through, and increasing war weariness, led the French to accept the Prussian terms for ending the war in January 1871.

The final episode of the war took place after the new German Empire had been created and the peace settlement had been agreed in March. Following the strain of the siege and the humiliation of defeat, radical revolutionaries seized power in Paris and established the Commune in defiance of the French government. Prussian forces continued to surround northern Paris but were otherwise not involved. In May, French troops loyal to the government recaptured Paris from the Commune, amid scenes of great violence and destruction. This finally ended the fighting but left a legacy of bitterness and political division within France. The experience of the war also left lasting hatred on both sides that resurfaced in 1914 at the start of the First World War.

Chronology

Background

The Franco-Prussian war

The Germans and the French

The new Germany created in 1871 called itself the Second Empire, or *Reich* in German; just as the Nazi German state of 1938–45 called itself the Third Reich or Greater Germany. Both laid claim to be the heirs of the original 'Holy Roman Empire of the German Peoples', the last and greatest of the medieval European empires, the origins of which stretched back to the 9th century, and which was dominated for most of the medieval period by the Habsburg rulers of Austria. By the 18th century, Austrian authority over this bewildering collection of more than 300 states, cities and principalities had become increasingly notional, contested both by the Kingdom of Prussia (part of which lay technically outside the old empire) and by France, the traditional enemy, which at its most ambitious saw the Rhine as its natural eastern frontier.

The Holy Roman Empire's end came in the upheavals of the French Revolution of 1789, the wars that began three years later, and the efforts, first of the French Republic and then of Napoleon Bonaparte, to overthrow the old order in Europe. Bonaparte proclaimed himself Emperor Napoleon of France in 1804, and two years later forced the last Holy Roman Emperor to relinquish the title and the vestiges of its formal authority, becoming Emperor of Austria (a title already in common use for about a century). In 1815 at the Congress of Vienna, part of the peace settlement ending the Napoleonic Wars, the complexities of the Holy Roman Empire were simplified into 39 independent states, of which the largest was Bavaria, all together forming with Austria and Prussia the loose political association of the German Confederation, with a parliament or assembly meeting in different cities as required. Until 1871, 'Germany' was chiefly a geographical

expression and a cultural idea, not unlike 'Europe' in the early 21st century.

Among the problems facing the rulers of Europe after 1815 was that another major war might well provoke a further revolution, giving rise to events like the 'Terror' of the Paris Revolutionary Commune of 1792–94. France was returned to essentially its pre-Revolution borders, and its monarchy was re-installed under King Louis XVIII – succeeded by King Charles X in 1824 – as first among equals with Austria and Prussia in Europe. Great Britain, although concerned about European affairs, was safe from invasion with the most powerful navy in the world, and increasingly preoccupied with its expanding colonial and trading empire. The Russian Empire, also, was concerned with its own expansion into Asia. European politics, including the threats or consequences of wars, were to be regulated by the Concert of Europe, an informal arrangement between these five 'Great Powers' to ensure that each was satisfied.

The Revolutionary and Napoleonic Wars of 1792–1815 had greatly strengthened the powerful beliefs of nationalism or patriotism that dominated Europe for the next two centuries. The Austrian Empire, which encompassed many non-German territories, including Hungary and parts of the Balkans and northern Italy, was particularly troubled by these nationalist movements. In contrast, early 19th-century France was Europe's most developed nation state as well as its most powerful. Revolutionary France had firmly established in Europe the idea of the patriotic citizen with rights and duties, which included fighting in what was called 'People's War'. In 1793, under threat of invasion, France had introduced both conscription (compulsory military service) for all young men, and the idea of

One of the many imaginative depictions of incidents in the war. French artillery in action in woodland during the siege of Paris. Painting by Edouard Detaille. (1848–1912). (AKG Berlin)

organising the entire society of the country for the war effort. Linked to nationalism, the other main ideological forces in 19th-century Europe were liberalism, including the belief that the old order must be reformed, which resulted in most monarchies also having some form of elected assembly with limited powers; and a growing radicalism, which at its extreme became the belief that the old order should simply be destroyed. Europe after 1815 also saw the rise of the political (and often religious) ideology of conservatism, which hoped to harness the energies of nationalism while avoiding either much greater reform or even revolution.

The Vienna Settlement lasted until 1830, when a series of political revolutions took place in Europe. Belgium became independent from the Netherlands, and in 1839 was guaranteed neutrality. In France, King Charles X abdicated and was replaced by his more liberal relative the Duke of Orléans, who became King Louis-Philippe, 'the citizen king', whose reign was known as the July Monarchy. Already divided by events since 1789, French political life including the higher commands of the French Army became further split between Republicans, Legitimist Royalists, Bonapartists and Orléanists.

In 1848, the year that Karl Marx (as an exile in London) published *The Communist Manifesto*, a second and much larger wave of revolts struck Europe. These uprisings, a mixture of liberalism, radicalism and nationalism, were mostly eventually suppressed, but often only in return for political reforms. The attitude and effectiveness of each country's army was also of critical importance in deciding the outcome. A successful revolution again took place in Paris, where King Louis-Philippe was deposed and the Second Republic created, with Louis Napoleon, the nephew of Emperor Napoleon I, as its president. In 1851, with the help of the army, Louis Napoleon overthrew the republic in a Paris coup to become 'Prince-President', and the next year proclaimed the Second Empire, with himself as Emperor Napoleon III (Bonapartists considered the son of Napoleon I, who had died in 1832 without ever ruling, to have been 'Napoleon II').

Nationalism in Europe was driven by social, cultural and economic forces as much

The Emperor Napoleon III. A contemporary French lithograph. (Ann Ronan Picture Library)

as by politics, in particular by the increasing impact of the industrial revolution. Although much of France and Germany remained agricultural, industry was on the rise, and both towns and wider populations were growing in size and importance. In the generation after 1815, the population of Prussia grew by more than half. Increasing middle-class wealth combined with literacy and cultural awareness into a new political importance for 'public opinion'. Attitudes and behaviour in Paris and Berlin, rather than the rest of France or Prussia, were what mattered in the revolutions of 1848, and both cities doubled in size over the next 30 years. By 1870 Paris, with a population of two million, rivalled London in importance; a building programme under Napoleon III, overseen by Baron Georges Haussman, created the great boulevards and many of the city's famous landmarks. Paris was the 'city of light', the cultural centre of Europe.

Industry was also beginning to transform warfare, in particular by steam-power with the development from the 1820s onwards of railways, coupled with the electric telegraph.

This promised a revolution in strategy by making the movement of large masses of troops across long distances possible in only days. New developments in metallurgy, electricity and chemistry were also having their impact with improved infantry and artillery weapons. By the 1850s the armies of most major powers were equipped with rifled muskets and field pieces, with a range, accuracy and effectiveness between two and three times as great as the weapons of 1815. The Prussian Army in 1848 adopted a breech-loading rifle, the Dreyse 'needle gun' (from its long needle-like firing-pin), a weapon some years ahead of its time. Increasingly fervent patriotism, larger populations, more rapid communications and greater firepower, all suggested new ways of war. This was the military aspect of the issue for European conservatives after 1848: how to harness this new nationalism and its warfighting power without risking 'People's War' and revolution.

The events of 1848–71 are usually called the 'Unification of Germany', but strictly it was not unified but split by excluding Austria, which was replaced by Prussia as the leader of the German world. German nationalists, like others elsewhere in Europe, argued both that their people had a right to a unified country, and that once the country had been unified they could then strengthen its nationhood, creating Germans as well as Germany. The debate was whether this meant a 'greater Germany' including the non-German peoples of the Austrian Empire, or a 'little Germany' based on Prussia, which from 1819 onwards established economic links throughout the German confederation by means of a Customs Union. The liberal Frankfurt Parliament of the German Confederation, meeting among the revolutions of 1848–49, offered the emperorship of a unified Germany to King Frederick William IV of Prussia, who declined and eventually sent troops to disperse the delegates. But Prussia's weaknesses were exposed in 1848–49, as part of the German Confederation in the First Schleswig-Holstein War against Denmark, being forced to make

peace by other European powers. When in 1850 Prussia tried to engineer the creation of a federal 'little Germany,' on its own terms, Austria threatened war, and in the 'humiliation of Olmütz' Prussia was again forced to back down. As a result of these upheavals Prussia also adopted a more liberal constitution in 1850.

Napoleon III, having come to power with the help of the army and the memory of French glory under Napoleon I, was determined to maintain and enhance France's position, recreating the trappings of empire, including the Imperial Guard. In 1818 France had introduced a system of limited conscription by ballot, which in 1851 produced an army of about 288,000 long-service troops. Recruits were not generally of high quality: men who got an 'unlucky number' in the ballot had to serve for seven years, but could pay a substitute to take their places, and over half of them did so, some even taking out insurance. Illiteracy in new conscripts ran at about 20–30 per cent, creating serious problems with training. A further intake, in theory liable to call-out in war, received no training at all until 1860, and then only a few months. By law, at least a third of officers had to be promoted from the ranks, and in practice more than half of all officers were ex-rankers. Regimental officers were a combination of older veterans and younger aristocrats, which often meant good military leadership at regimental level but produced political divisions at the level of generals. Regiments had depots spread throughout France (and in Algeria and Corsica, which were governed as part of France), but were moved between garrison towns around the country to prevent political problems. In 1870 only 36 out of 100 regiments of the infantry of the line were garrisoned in their depot towns. The French Army joked that it operated under *Le Système D* for *'Débrouillage'*, meaning improvisation or muddling through, and its supplies and communications were often chaotic. But this was not much different from the army of Napoleon I, or any other army in Europe or elsewhere before 1870. After its defeat by the

Prussians almost everything about the French Army was portrayed as wrong or foolish. But having to balance the needs of political reliability at home and wars both in Europe and in France's colonial possessions, it had a long record of success against a number of different opponents.

Napoleon III needed military glory and success to maintain his own position, both with the army itself and with Paris public opinion. The French Army was victorious in the Crimean War of 1854–56, in alliance with the British, the Ottoman Turkish Empire and the Kingdom of Sardinia (or Piedmont) against the Russians. In the Franco-Austrian War of 1859, fought in northern Italy in alliance with Sardinia, it inflicted a major defeat on the Austrians, and also made the first significant use of railways for deployment in war. The Italians spoke of the *Furia francese* ('French fury'), particularly the speed and power of the French infantry charge. In 1860 the French also fought successfully alongside the British in the Second Opium War in China. France of the Second Empire set the model for armies throughout the globe. In particular, the tactics and fighting methods – and uniforms – of the American Civil War of 1861–65 were based on those of France. The demands of the Civil War also prevented the United States from acting on its traditional hostility to European involvement in the Americas. Taking advantage of this Napoleon III sent troops to intervene in the continuing civil war in Mexico in 1861, attempting to establish French rule. In 1864 the Austrian Archduke Maximilian was proclaimed Emperor of Mexico by Napoleon. But France had overreached itself; and when the American Civil War ended Napoleon abandoned Maximilian, who was captured and shot by a Mexican firing squad in 1867.

With its global interests and long-standing rivalry with Great Britain (which was persistently afraid of invasion), France had one of the largest and best navies in the world, also being transformed by the impact of steam power. The French warship *La Gloire*, launched in 1859 and powered by steam and sail with her wooden sides protected by iron

King Wilhelm I of Prussia. A contemporary engraving from about the time that he came to the throne in 1861. (Ann Ronan Picture Library)

plates, qualified as the world's first 'ironclad'. By 1870 the French Navy included 49 ironclad warships, compared with only five ironclads and about 30 other vessels in the Prussian Navy. France also had extensive international trade and an important merchant marine fleet. Although the Franco-Prussian War would not be a naval war, this French strength in seapower would have important consequences for its conduct.

In both the Crimean War and the Franco-Austrian War, all sides were careful to end the fighting quickly and not to claim too much in the peace settlement. The potential risks of engaging in even these limited conflicts and in harnessing nationalism for war were demonstrated for conservatives in 1860–61, just after the Austrian defeat. An attempt to unite the northern and central Italian states fused with the actions of southern nationalist forces under the revolutionary Giuseppe Garibaldi in confused fighting that produced a unified Kingdom of Italy. The new state lacked only Austrian Venetia, and also Rome, where the

presence of two French regiments (first sent in 1849) allowed the Pope to keep his authority. A unified Italy was an important symbol for nationalists throughout Europe.

The next challenge to the French ranking in Europe came from Prussia, which in 1850 had seemed the weakest of the Great Powers. In 1857 King Frederick William IV became incapable of ruling. His brother was made regent, and in 1861 succeeded as King William I – his name is usually given in its German form as 'Wilhelm'. Next year King Wilhelm appointed Count Otto von Bismarck as his minister-president (or prime minister). The

Prussian Army stood at about 130,000 soldiers, made up chiefly of three-year conscripts. The Prussian version of 'People's War' against Napoleon I had been the creation in 1813 of a large compulsory militia, the *Landwehr*. Officered largely by the middle classes, the Landwehr could still be called out to fight, and was seen as a liberal counterweight to the conservative politics of the Prussian Army.

In 1858 General Helmuth von Moltke was appointed Chief of the Prussian General Staff,

A Prussian Landwehr infantry regiment. Wood engraving, September 1870. (Ann Ronan Picture Library)

and next year General Albrecht von Roon was made minister for war. General Roon, who saw the Prussian Army and its values as central to any national aspirations, planned for a considerably increased army supported by placing the Landwehr completely under army control. This fitted Bismarck's political plans for defeating his liberal opponents. By 1863 the implementation of Roon's plan had produced a political crisis, which King Wilhelm resolved on Bismarck's advice by dissolving the Prussian Assembly rather than let it block the military reforms. Moltke concentrated on establishing his General Staff as a technically professional elite, dealing with how to recall large numbers of reservists quickly in case of war, and creating a special railway section to plan transporting the forces by rail to their locations. Under Moltke, General Staff officers became known in the Prussian Army by the nickname 'Demigods,' with no great affection.

In 1864 the reforms to the Prussian Army were put to their first test in the renewed conflict with Denmark over the future of the duchies of Schleswig and Holstein. The Second Schleswig-Holstein War was a brief and complete success for the forces of the German Confederation, led by Prussia and Austria. A dispute over the future government of the duchies, largely engineered by Bismarck, then provided the pretext for the Austro-Prussian War of 1866. Saxony allied itself with Austria, while most of the German Confederation states fought alongside Prussia. Italy also sided with Prussia, tying down Austrian forces in the south. Using railways to deploy, the Prussians invaded Austria and inflicted a crushing defeat in July in the war's only major battle at Königgrätz (also known as the battle of Sadowa). Moltke's desire to march into Vienna was restrained by Bismarck, who needed a quick end to the war.

The victory in the 'Seven Weeks War' more than restored Prussia's political and military reputation. In Prussia itself, new elections produced an Assembly dominated by conservatives under Bismarck. The rest of Europe was stunned by the speed and completeness of the Austrian defeat. Most

commentators pointed to the superiority of the Dreyse needle gun over the Austrian muzzle-loading rifles as the decisive factor. Some noted the impact of railways, and the effectiveness of the Prussian staffwork. But the root causes of the Prussian victory were Bismarck's political skill in fighting an isolated enemy and then ending the war swiftly, coupled with Moltke's skill in military bureaucracy and administration; and above all the attitude of the Prussian people in accepting a large conscript army as an essential part of their national identity, and their patriotic willingness to subordinate themselves to its fierce discipline and fight for their country.

Following the Peace of Prague which ended the war the German Confederation was dissolved, and in 1867 a new North German Confederation was created under Prussia, excluding Austria. Together with outright annexations of some smaller German states, this in effect doubled the size of Prussia. The remaining southern German states, Bavaria, Württemberg and Baden, signed agreements with Prussia including a secret military alliance which would be activated in 1870. Austria paid an indemnity and gave up Venetia to Italy. The defeat also led to self-rule for Hungary within the Austrian Empire, which renamed itself the Dual Monarchy of Austria–Hungary in 1867. Otherwise, both the shock of the quick defeat and the moderate peace settlement limited any Austrian desire for a future war against Prussia.

The glittering Great Exhibition in Paris in 1867 marked the high point of Second Empire prestige. But Paris was not only the centre of European culture, it was also home to every shade of political opinion from anarchists and 'Reds' (a traditional name for revolutionaries) to authoritarian ultra-Monarchists. In 1869 Napoleon III announced a more liberal constitution, and the new government under Premier Emile Olliver advocated peace and even disarmament. Napoleon had suffered one setback in Mexico, and was not necessarily seeking a war. But continuing to portray itself as the most important country in Europe, France neither could, nor would, ignore the Prussian challenge.

The nations in arms

King Wilhelm I of Prussia, as the ruler of his country and commander-in-chief of the Prussian Army, was far from being a figurehead. Born in 1797, he was dignified and courteous, deeply conservative in politics, and like most of his subjects a devout Protestant. It was nothing unusual in the Franco-Prussian War for his soldiers to break into a solemn hymn on occasions of celebration. King Wilhelm was also the head of the Hohenzollern family, which had ruled Prussia since its creation in the 17th century and had branches and marriage connections throughout Europe. He had fought against Napoleon I in 1814 and been awarded the Iron Cross. He saw both kingship and command as a duty, and his Royal Headquarters accompanied the Prussian Army into the field in 1870, including courtiers and princes, war reporters and other functionaries from several countries, as well as Bismarck's political staff. King Wilhelm's relations with his minister-president were complex, as in any constitutional monarchy of the era. The most able and ruthless European statesman of his day, Count Otto von Bismarck-Schönhausen was 55 years old in 1870. He accompanied the Royal Headquarters wearing the major general's uniform to which he was officially entitled, and dominated the politics of the war. This inevitably produced disputes between Bismarck and Moltke as Chief of the Prussian General Staff about where the boundaries of political control and military necessity lay.

At 70 years old, General Moltke had already tried to retire once. Like surprisingly many other able German generals, he was not from a traditional Prussian *Junker* (aristocratic) family. Although German-speaking, he was born in Denmark and transferred from the Danish Army to the Prussian Army in 1822.

As a full-time career staff officer, until he led the Prussian Army into war in 1866 he had never commanded a military unit of any size. His great achievement was the establishment of the Prussian General Staff as a technical and administrative elite carrying out detailed peacetime planning for future wars, that later became a model for the rest of the world. Also, under Moltke the chief of staff at each

A contemporary picture of Otto von Bismarck in his military uniform. (Ann Ronan Picture Library)

level, as the General Staff representative, held equal – and sometimes greater – authority than the formation commander.

The officers of the Prussian Army were a tight-knit group. About half of all officers, and most of the senior ranks, were Prussian Junkers for who soldiering was a career: in the campaign of 1870, two brothers from the aristocratic von Alvensleben family commanded III Corps and IV Corps respectively of the Prussian Second Army; Bismarck's own sons, Herbert and Wilhelm, both served as officers with the Prussian cavalry. In 1866 Moltke had established with Wilhelm I his own right to issue orders directly, but this idea of professionalism rather than of the aristocratic right of command was not yet completely accepted. Moltke's greatest problems in 1870 came from General Karl von Steinmetz commanding the Prussian First Army, a much-decorated 74-year-old veteran who like King Wilhelm had begun his career fighting Napoleon I. Although only 39 years old, Crown Prince Frederick William of Prussia commanded Third Army, and his 42-year-old cousin, Prince Frederick Charles of Prussia (the 'Red Prince' from his distinctive red Hussar uniform), commanded Second Army.

In the Franco-Prussian War, Moltke commanded what was officially the Federal Army of the North German Confederation and its allies, although since 1867 the Prussian system had been extended to all the forces involved. Conscripts entered the army at 20 years old and served for three years (four years with the cavalry and artillery) before returning to civilian life, remaining with the reserve for four years and the Landwehr for another five. Even with the much larger intake than France, the quality of troops was higher and illiteracy among Prussian conscripts was almost unknown. In wartime the reserve and the first year of the Landwehr (all men up to 28 years old) could be immediately recalled for service, while the remaining Landwehr could be activated as a reserve force. This gave Moltke in 1870 a Prussian field army of 730,000 men.

The Prussian Army structure in 1870 was similar to that of any large European-style army. Its basis was the army corps, a force of all arms of about 30,000 men, equipped and organised to function and fight on its own if necessary, like a small army. There were 13 of these army corps, of which all but two were each based on a district of Prussia, and consisted of two infantry divisions. A typical division had two brigades, made up of two regiments with three battalions each, plus a divisional battalion of *Jäger* (light infantry), a cavalry regiment and divisional artillery. The exceptions were the Prussian Guard Corps, which also had three cavalry brigades, and XII Royal Saxon Corps which included 12th Cavalry Division; 25th (Hessian) Division, part of IX Corps, also had a slightly different divisional structure (four regiments of two battalions each plus the artillery). The remaining six cavalry divisions (formed of two brigades, each brigade coming from an army corps area) were allocated to army corps as needed, or grouped as a reserve. Although there was much variation in uniform, most troops wore the Prussian dark-blue tunic and spiked *Pickelhaube* helmet, and carried the 1860 or 1862 model of the Dreyse breech-loader. Bavaria contributed its own I and II Bavarian Corps, with a distinctive lighter blue uniform and crested helmet, mostly carrying the Podwill rifle (converted from muzzle-loader to breech-loader) or the newer Werder rifle rather than the Dreyse. Württemberg and Baden each contributed an independent division.

Like his Prussian opposite, Emperor Napoleon III was both ruler of his country and commander-in-chief. Born in 1808, he was an intelligent, emotional man, never easy to understand or explain. The son of Hortense Beauharnais and Louis Bonaparte (brother of Napoleon I and King of Holland 1806–10), he lived in exile after 1815, and became leader of the Bonapartists in 1832. Twice, in 1836 and 1840, he had led failed coups in France, before his success in 1848–51. He commanded the French Army personally in the Franco-Austrian War, but in 1870 his health was failing and he was in

Helmuth von Moltke. A tinted lithograph c. 1880 showing him after his elevation to field marshal and to count as a reward for his victories in the war. (Ann Ronan Picture Library)

great pain, particularly with gallstones in his bladder. Nevertheless, his position and the myth of Napoleon I as a great war-leader compelled him to take command. The disastrous result was that he could not lead effectively himself, while his presence with the army made it almost impossible for anyone else to do so. There was no equivalent on the French side of Moltke and the General Staff, or of Bismarck. Napoleon left behind in Paris, in addition to Premier Olliver, a regency council headed by his wife, the Empress Eugénie, a former Spanish countess and a devout Catholic who loathed both liberalism and Prussia equally.

Again unlike their Prussian opposites, the remaining French leaders changed according to the fortunes of the war. In its early phase the two most important French military commanders were Marshal François-Achille Bazaine and Marshal Patrice Count de

The Empress Eugénie. A portrait by Franz Xavier Winterhalter. (1806–73).
(Ann Ronan Picture Library)

MacMahon the Duke of Magenta,
respectively commanders of the Army of the
Rhine and the Army of Châlons, who
represented very different factions in the
politics of the French Army, but who were
also experienced and competent soldiers with
high reputations. Bazaine was born in 1811
at Versailles, the son of a French soldier from
a village near Metz who then deserted his
family to enter Russian service. In 1831,
having failed the examinations to become an
officer, Bazaine enlisted in the ranks of the
infantry. In 1833 he transferred to the
Foreign Legion, rising to become a colonel by
1852. Bazaine continued to distinguish
himself in the Crimea, in Italy and in
Mexico, being made a marshal of France and
the Emperor Maximilian's military
commander in 1864. It was unusual for an
ex-ranker to rise so high, and Bazaine was
naturally popular with Republicans, but

Bavarian infantry attacking a French fort during the
Franco-Prussian War. (Ann Ronan Picture Library)

sometimes over-deferential to his aristocratic
fellow generals. In contrast to Bazaine,
Marshal MacMahon (from an originally Irish
family that had settled in France in the
17th century) was an aristocrat and a
Legitimist Monarchist whose father had been
ennobled by King Charles X. Born in 1808 in
Sully (near Dijon), MacMahon had begun his
career as an officer in 1827. He had also
distinguished himself in the Crimea before
entering politics, had commanded an army
corps in Italy in 1859 for which he was
promoted to marshal, and had represented
France at King Wilhelm I's coronation in
Prussia. Much more a 'political general' than
Bazaine, he was recalled in 1870 from Algeria,
where his appointment as governor-general
had proved controversial.

France after the Austro-Prussian War was not particularly conscious of any great military weakness compared to Prussia, but recognised that changes had to be made. If it came to war, a French Army of 288,000 was just too small. But most French liberal politicians, seeing that an alliance of generals with conservatives had destroyed liberal hopes in Prussia, opposed any extension of conscription or increase in the political power of the French Army; most conservatives opposed the higher taxes needed to pay for the reforms; and few except Bonapartists wanted more power for Napoleon III. The result in 1868 was a compromise between the competing interests of French politics and within the army itself. Conscript service was reduced, but only to five years, with substitution still allowed. Although the intake of conscripts was increased, half of those taken were only required to serve for five months, training over a three-year period. Those who completed their five years with the army went into a new reserve for a further four years. An attempt was also made to form an equivalent of the Landwehr in a revival of the National Guard, created in the days of the Revolution, which was to be divided into static (or 'sedentary') local National Guard forces and a *Garde National Mobile*, often called just the *Garde Mobile*. In theory the National Guard included all able-bodied men who were not otherwise conscripted, plus the reserves who had completed their four years, but political pressure limited Garde Mobile training to no more than 14 non-consecutive days a year for five years, the supposed 'guardsmen' returning home each night. These reforms were meant to produce a wartime Army of 800,000 plus 400,000 Garde Mobile by 1875; but had little time to take effect before July 1870, when the active field army stood at about 377,000, plus a largely untrained reserve of 173,000 more, and a Garde Mobile that existed chiefly on paper.

French Army organisation was similar to that of Prussia, being also based on the army corps. The Army of the Rhine, which at the start of the war constituted the effective field army of France, had eight army corps of which one was the Imperial Guard Corps, together with a cavalry reserve of four divisions. A typical army corps was three infantry divisions and a cavalry division, but some stronger army corps had an extra infantry division. Infantry divisions usually consisted of two brigades, each with two regiments of three battalions, plus a *chasseur* (light infantry) battalion and the divisional artillery. French divisions had no fixed separate numbers, and were usually known by their commander's name. The Imperial Guard Corps had instead a Voltigeur Division of two brigades (*voltigeur* was a term for elite light infantry), a Grenadier Division of two brigades, and a Guard Cavalry Division, plus the Guard Artillery. Some French uniforms were famously colourful and picturesque, particularly among the infantry and cavalry of the *Armée d'Afrique*, recruited from Algerians and other North Africans, but most French infantry wore their traditional red trousers and red *képi* (peaked cap) with a dark blue tunic.

Because most soldiers on both sides wore essentially the same dark blue, and many uniforms were unfamiliar to either, there was often confusion both with reports of friends as enemies, and with troops failing to fire at the enemy or firing at their own side. The infantry of the Württemberg Division, for example, wore a blue *képi* in 1870, while on the French side many soldiers even in the first month of the war had no proper uniforms. This issue of what constituted a uniform became important in the later stages of the war, when disputes arose over whether the French were arming civilians. But as early as August 1870, even some Prussian troops were taking French uniforms and equipment to replace their own as they wore out.

In general terms of populations, economies, size and strength, the balance between France and the Prussian-led North German Confederation favoured France. There was no obvious Prussian advantage; if it came to war everything depended on how well the two rivals could translate their respective underlying strengths into military force, and how well they could fight.

The Ems telegram

Bismarck's exact role in provoking the Franco-Prussian War has always been a matter of dispute, not least because he deceived both King Wilhelm and others at the time, and then lied in his memoirs; but there is no doubt that his actions caused its outbreak. Bismarck was interested in increasing Prussia's power, but not necessarily in a Greater Germany or in a war with France. The southern German states, with a more liberal tradition than Prussia, had little desire to lose their independence, particularly in the case of Catholic Bavaria. But these issues could be solved if France declared war on Prussia, and Prussia could be made to seem the innocent party. Moltke had created the perfect instrument for winning short, aggressive wars; and Bismarck had no scruples at all about using it. When the war broke out, almost all Germans and the rest of Europe blamed it on French aggression and recklessness, and on Napoleon III personally.

The behaviour of France, and of Napoleon III himself, defies any simple explanation. The Second Empire proclaimed itself as committed to peace, but at the same time Napoleon spoke of the grandeur of France and denounced the limitations of the 1815 Vienna settlement. The transfer of frontier provinces (whose inhabitants often had a mixed language and culture) from one country to another could still take place, despite the growing strength of nationalism; and as part of its reward for defeating Austria in 1859 France had gained Savoy from its ally the Kingdom of Sardinia. In 1866, France intervened politically in the Austro-Prussian War, expecting to make territorial gains in return for staying neutral. In two related French attempts, Bismarck made vague promises that France might absorb the Duchy of Luxemburg (of which the King of the

Netherlands was also ruler, but which contained Prussian troops), and even parts of the Prussian and Bavarian lands known by their medieval name as the Rhine Palatinate. When this leaked out in the 'Luxemburg Crisis', southern German nationalists demanded war with France, Bismarck denounced the whole idea and the British were outraged. At the 1867 London Conference, called to resolve the issue, Luxemburg was declared perpetually independent and neutral. In the same year that its empire in Mexico collapsed, France ended up with nothing except the feeling that it had been cheated. French public opinion swung further not only against Prussia, but also against Napoleon's government.

In this political climate almost any episode might have led to war, but the next crisis had a strange origin. In September 1868 the last ruler of Spain from the House of Bourbon, Queen Isabella II, was overthrown in a revolt, the 'Glorious Revolution', and fled to France. The Spaniards established a more liberal constitution, and sought a suitable candidate for a constitutional monarchy among the royal houses of Europe. Their preferred choice was Leopold, the eldest son of Prince Karl Anton of Hohenzollern-Sigmaringen, the Catholic branch of the Hohenzollern family headed by King Wilhelm of Prussia. Prince Karl Anton had also been Prussia's minister-president before Bismarck, Prince Leopold was married to the daughter of the king of Portugal, and one of his brothers was ruler – later King Carol I – of Rumania.

While this was happening, France was negotiating with Austria–Hungary and Italy on the assumption that either country, or even both, would readily join it as allies against Prussia in a future war, despite the Austrians' reaction to their defeat in 1866,

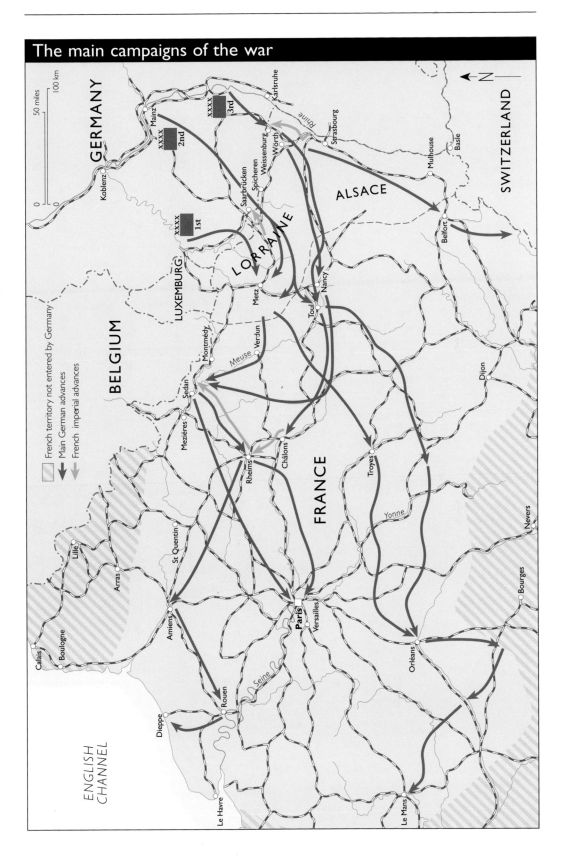

The main campaigns of the war

GERMANY

SWITZERLAND

BELGIUM

LUXEMBURG

ALSACE

LORRAINE

FRANCE

ENGLISH CHANNEL

Koblenz

Mainz

Karlsruhe

Saarbrücken

Spicheren

Weissenburg

Wörth

Strasbourg

Mulhouse

Basle

Belfort

Metz

Nancy

Toul

Montmédy

Verdun

Meuse

Sedan

Mezières

Rheims

Châlons

Dijon

Troyes

Yonne

Nevers

St Quentin

Lille

Arras

Amiens

Paris

Versailles

Orléans

Bourges

Calais

Boulogne

Dieppe

Rouen

Seine

Le Havre

Le Mans

Rhine

XXXX 2nd

XXXX 3rd

XXXX 1st

50 miles

100 km

0

0

N

French territory not entered by Germany

Main German advances

French imperial advances

KÖNIGSSTRASSE

PEACE—AND NO PIECES!

Bismarck: 'Pardon, Mon Ami, but we really can't allow you to pick up anything here.' Nap (the Chiffonier): 'Pray don't mention it M'sieu. It's not of the slightest consequence.' A cartoon by John Tenniel from *Punch*, 25 August 1866, depicting Napoleon III as a chiffonier (rag-collector), and reflecting France's attempts to make territorial gains from the Austro-Prussian War. (Ann Ronan Picture Library)

and the fact that Austria–Hungary and Italy were rivals and enemies (there were also the physical difficulties in getting Italian troops to the Prussian frontier, and the problem that French troops were preventing Rome from becoming part of a united Italy). Discussions even took place with Denmark over a possible French amphibious landing in the Baltic. Negotiations and vague promises led to nothing by the war's outbreak. Of the other great powers, Russia was not involved, while Great Britain viewed France as its main rival and, given Napoleon III's behaviour, as its most likely future enemy in a war. Meanwhile, Prussia's own alliance with the southern German states under the secret clauses of the Peace of Prague was secure. On the outbreak of the war, a French army corps was even assembled on the Pyrenees, in case Spain also joined the war on the Prussian side. Like Austria in 1866, France was diplomatically isolated.

In April 1870 Spain began the delicate process of offering Prince Leopold the crown, something which required the assent of King Wilhelm as head of the Hohenzollern family. Usually this would have been a normal part of European dynastic diplomacy. But France at once reacted with great hostility, both at the idea that it had not been consulted, and at the prospect of a possible ally of Prussia as ruler of Spain. Both Leopold and his younger brother Frederick signalled their refusal of the Spanish offer; but Bismarck, suffering from frequent illnesses but intent on confrontation with France, persuaded King Wilhelm to support the Hohenzollern candidature without letting France into the negotiations. There was no formal contact between the French government and that of Prussia, which was not officially involved. But both the Spanish offer and the French attitude became common knowledge, and on 2 July when the news broke in the Paris press, Prince Karl Anton and his son were placed in a very difficult position.

In May, a plebiscite in France had overwhelmingly confirmed the new liberal constitution, giving Napoleon III and his government enhanced political authority as the 'Liberal Empire'. The Council of Ministers and members (known as deputies) of the new Legislative Assembly spoke grandly of how the honour of France had been insulted. Prussia must be forced to back down. On 6 July, Foreign Minister Duke

Agénor de Gramont addressed the Assembly with a public statement from the council that France would pursue 'peace if that is possible, [but] war if that is inevitable' to prevent the Hohenzollern candidature. The French Army began to implement its preliminary war plans. Bismarck at once took steps to further rouse Prussian public opinion against France through the press, and the Prussian Army also began to take its first actions for war.

On 9 July the French ambassador to Prussia, Count Vincente Benedetti, obtained the first of several meetings with King Wilhelm, who was taking a rest cure at the spa of Bad Ems, near Koblenz in the Palatinate, demanding in the name of France that he withdrew Leopold's candidacy. King Wilhelm spoke fluent French, the international language of the European aristocracy and of diplomacy, and the meetings were courteous and even friendly. Benedetti was also in frequent – although sometimes garbled – contact with Paris through the telegraph. Meanwhile rumours and reports of war preparations on both sides passed between diplomats in Paris and Berlin.

From his first meeting with Benedetti, King Wilhelm made what was for him the crucial distinction that he was involved privately and personally as head of the Hohenzollerns, but not as the head of the Prussian government. As the crisis deepened, on 12 July Prince Karl Anton announced that his son Leopold (who was unreachable, taking a walking holiday in the Alps) had withdrawn his candidacy. This was proclaimed in Paris as the Prussian defeat that Napoleon needed, but the clamour was for even more. Benedetti was ordered to demand from King Wilhelm a guarantee that Leopold would never accept the Spanish throne, and an apology for the insult to France. At their last meeting, while walking in a park on the morning of 13 July, King Wilhelm politely declined to do this, and equally correctly declined further official contact with the ambassador since the affair was over, although seeing Benedetti onto his train as he had been recalled to Paris. The king then sent a diplomatic telegram describing the meeting to Berlin, where Bismarck was in consultation with Moltke and Roon, the minister for war.

Napoleon and his Council of Ministers, already divided over their best course of action, had decided not to press this issue, and the affair could have ended with a successfully manufactured French diplomatic triumph. Bismarck averted this by exploiting both the speed of the telegraph and public opinion. The original report of King Wilhelm's last contact with Benedetti had been an accurate account of a respectful meeting. Bismarck prepared a shorter, redrafted version which became famous as the 'Ems Telegram', stating that after the French ambassador's demands 'His Majesty the King thereupon refused to receive the ambassador again and through his adjutant informed the ambassador that he had nothing further to say', and released this to the press. It appeared in Berlin newspapers that evening.

Next day was 14 July, Bastille Day, the French national day with a military parade through the centre of Paris, and Bismarck's version of the Ems Telegram was in newspapers across Europe, including the main Paris journals. Foreign Minister

Gramont told Olliver that the treatment of Benedetti was an insult that France could not tolerate, while in both capital cities crowds in the streets demanded war. Again it was the attitude of Paris that mattered rather than the provinces of France, where the idea of war was greeted generally with acceptance rather than great enthusiasm. The Council of Ministers was still divided, but after some debate Napoleon ordered the call-up of the reserves. Next day the Assembly was asked to vote the money for a war against Prussia. Olliver told the deputies that he accepted responsibility 'with a light heart', meaning (as he always afterwards insisted) that he was confident and that his conscience was clear. In another phrase that afterwards stuck in French throats, Marshal Edmond Leboeuf, the minister for war, was reported as declaring the French Army ready 'to the last gaiter button'. The assembly voted overwhelmingly, 245 to 10, in favour.

When news of this reached Berlin, Moltke was authorised to implement his war plans on 16 July. The formal French declaration of war, transmitted to Berlin next day and delivered to Bismarck on 19 July, was the first official communication between the two governments since the crisis had started.

The invasion of France

Both sides expected the French to attack first, invading from France's eastern provinces of Alsace and Lorraine across the common frontier into the Palatinate. Given that the assembled Federal Army would be much larger than any French Army that could take the field, this was France's main chance for a victory; and France had, after all, both sought and declared war. The railway system in France was also superior to that of Prussia, in which the General Staff's control over railways in wartime had not yet been fully established. A French invasion and an initial Prussian defeat could force Bavaria and the southern states into neutrality, and bring Austria or Italy into the war on the French side. Such an expansion of the war might also involve the British politically, ending it in the French favour.

In fact the French were completely unprepared to take any such action, and their only plans for war with Prussia were rudimentary. The Franco-Prussian War was later identified as the only case that century in which a country had declared war with no prior preparation or military action. But the Prussians did not know that, and Moltke had based his own plans on the urgent need to get as many troops to the frontier as fast as possible, even leaving the supply trains behind at first to increase the number of combat soldiers. His worst-case assessment was that the French might attack with a force of about 150,000 by 25 July, slicing through the unprepared Prussians; if they had not done so by 1 August he believed that he could win a defensive campaign, and if they still had not attacked by 4 August he would take the offensive. A lot of what happened in the first two months of the war stemmed from the reasonable Prussian belief that the French Army and its generals, belonging to the most powerful country in

Europe, were at least as good as themselves. No-one on either side was prepared for just how badly the French were going to fare and even afterwards it remained hard to explain.

Three major military problems faced European generals at war in the mid-19th century. The first was the movement and supply of the vast new armies, both by rail and then on foot once they left their railheads. The forces mobilised on both sides in the Franco-Prussian War together constituted by far the largest armies in Europe that century. Not only was ammunition needed, but also thousands of horses for transport and haulage, and both horses and men required daily food and water. The second problem was how to communicate and exercise command over such large formations, both before and during the battle. The final problem was how to respond to the growing lethality of artillery and infantry firepower. Although they were known to be increasingly vulnerable, close troop formations were still needed to keep control and transmit orders, both when marching and on the battlefield.

The French had some experience of railways from 1859, but the lack of a proper General Staff or detailed peacetime preparation was a great handicap. Once away from the railheads, armies moved on foot as their ancestors had done, averaging about 10 miles (16 km) a day in 1870. Under Napoleon I the French Army had developed the technique of army corps moving separately across country for speed of manoeuvre and ease of supply, either through supply lines from depots or from the local countryside, or both. Given the limitations of 19th century roads, the army corps moved side by side, only coming together for a major battle. The military aphorism was 'separate to move, unite to fight'. Command of the new mass armies was seen as requiring essentially the same methods.

The issue of firepower had been addressed in the 1850s by the French 'chasseur school' of military thought, whose ideas spread throughout Europe. If weapons were three times as effective, then troops must advance in battle at three times the speed, at a fast trot or jog rather than walking, in more loose formations. This approach needed better recruits with higher levels of training, higher standards of fitness, and officers with a concern for the well-being of their men. Given that good recruits were not always available other French generals, particularly with engineering experience, preferred taking up strong defensive positions and tempting the enemy to advance into a hail of fire. Defensive entrenchments in the form of 'rifle pits,' holding up to 12 men, and the use of buildings as strongpoints, were not unusual. Regardless, the war would be won by brilliant French generalship and by *L'élan et le cran* – flair and guts.

The approach of the Prussian General Staff under Moltke to the same problems was altogether different, including a belief that the nature of generalship had changed. The Prussian Army in 1870 introduced two new words into the military vocabulary: 'mobilisation' meaning the rapid assembly of a mass army, and 'concentration', its equally rapid transport to the frontiers ready to fight. Moltke envisaged a single continuous movement, from the order to mobilise through to the concentration of the armies, the first encounters with the enemy, and the decisive victory in battle. Moltke did not expect to be able to control these events, and the field General Staff that he took with him as part of the Royal Headquarters was tiny: only 14 officers and 76 soldiers. Two of his often-quoted aphorisms were 'mistakes made in the initial deployment cannot be corrected', and 'no plan of operations extends with certainty beyond the first encounter with the enemy's main strength'. The war would be decided largely by greater numbers and Prussian staff training, and

won by the side that made the fewest mistakes. Victory in battle would depend on superior Prussian discipline, and on an overwhelming 'will to win'.

The Prussian emphasis on priority for fighting troops produced its own problems. Getting the balance right between troops and supplies had no obvious solution, and the armies while concentrating were extremely vulnerable to attack. Drawing on the Prussian tradition dating back to General Carl von Clausewitz (who died in 1831), Moltke argued that any such troubles would be resolved by defeating the enemy in battle. His preferred solution to the difficulty of attacking into increasing firepower was to make it the enemy's problem. As the dispersed army corps encountered the French, so they would curl in like the closing fingers of a hand to surround them, forcing the enemy to fight their way through the encirclement, and destroying themselves in a 'battle of annihilation'.

Unlike the wars of Napoleon I, which had been fought by armies with very similar weapons to each other, this was also a war in which weapons technology made a major difference to the way that both sides fought. In 1870 the famed Dreyse needle gun, with an effective range of 600 m, was nearly obsolete. In 1868, as part of their reforms, the French Army was equipped with a rifle of the next generation, the excellent Chassepot breech-loader, with a range of 1,500 m. Smokeless powder for both rifles and artillery was more than a decade in the future, and the clouds of smoke plus the need for close formations on the battlefield provided mass targets easily visible at the Chassepot's maximum range.

If the French were a generation ahead in rifles, the Prussians had a similar advantage in artillery. After encountering the very good Austrian artillery in 1866, they had re-equipped with the latest Krupp-built steel rifled breech-loaders with percussion-fused shells that burst on impact. There were two main calibres of field artillery: the '4-pdr' field gun (actually of 9 lb or just under 80 mm calibre) which equipped both the field artillery and horse artillery, and the '6-pdr' field gun (15 lb or 90 mm calibre); the maximum range of the 6 lb piece was 4,600 m. In practice field guns on both sides seldom opened fire at above 3,000 m, which was their effective range. The impressive Prussian train of siege artillery, of up to 210 mm calibres with ranges of between 4,000 m and 8,000 m, was of a similar high quality. The French had not had the time or money to modernise their artillery. They still used muzzle-loading bronze cannon, chiefly the 1858 pattern rifled 4-pdr calibre field gun with an upper range of 3,300 m, and the 1839 pattern 12-pdr smoothbore siege gun converted to rifling (the '12 pounder Napoleon' of American Civil War fame), with a notional upper range of 5,600 m. As a further disadvantage, these had only time-fused shells that burst at restricted pre-set ranges. French factories did not produce sufficient percussion fuses until after the war's start, and not until November 1870 could French artillery hold its own against the Prussians. The French artillery also included batteries of the *Mitrailleuse*, an early

machine gun mounted on wheels and treated as the equivalent of a field gun that could fire 125 rounds a minute out to about 2,500 m. Contrary to one common myth of the war this was a very effective weapon that the Prussians greatly respected.

The cavalry on both sides had serious problems: generals tended to underrate them, and they were badly used. For almost 20 years cavalry had been told that they were obsolete, since their horses could not survive the increases in firepower. But there was nothing that could replace cavalry in their two main functions of scouting for information, which with the new large armies was of increasingly greater importance, and making a mounted charge on the battlefield to scatter the enemy. Again after their experience in 1866 fighting

A French popular print depicting an incident at the battle of Gravelotte-St Privat. It shows a dismounted French dragoon using his carbine to shoot down a charging Prussian Uhlan (lancer), while French dragoons charge in the background. The original caption claims that, although wounded, the dragoon killed 12–15 Prussians with his carbine. (Ann Ronan Picture Library)

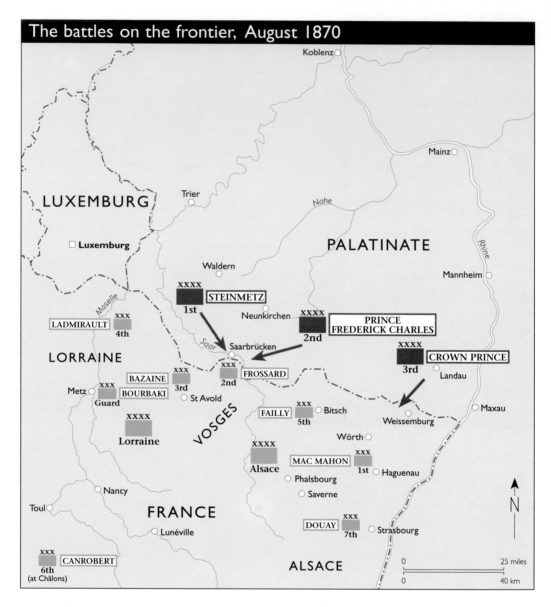

The battles on the frontier, August 1870

superior Austrian cavalry, the Prussian cavalry were rather better than the French at scouting, but the difficulties in getting the information back was one reason why Moltke believed that detailed planning was impossible, and why the armies often marched blindly about the countryside.

These differences in weapons between the two sides meant that battles took the form either of Prussian infantry taking heavy casualties trying to close the gap between the range of the Chassepot rifle and the Dreyse, or of French infantry duelling at long range

against Prussian artillery while the Prussian infantry hung back. In fact both sides' infantry were more reluctant to move to close range than their commanders liked, although not for lack of courage. Cavalry was still used to charge in battle, chiefly to disrupt enemy fire by presenting a second target in order to save infantry in trouble, rather than with any hope of a decisive effect. Again, the Prussians were better at choosing their moment than the French, who often threw away their cavalry in hopeless charges. Although some French and

The fighting   35

all Prussian cavalry carried breech-loading carbines (shortened rifles), neither had adopted the dismounted tactics combined with the charge seen in the later stages of the American Civil War.

The Prussian mobilisation and concentration was dictated largely by the shape of their railway system. The General Staff plans, drawn up over the winter of 1869–70, provided for the three armies to assemble along the Rhine between Koblenz in the north and Karlsruhe in the south, intending to envelop the French from both sides if they attacked eastwards into the Palatinate. Prussian regiments were mostly regionally based, with each parish recruiting a battalion; on mobilisation reserves returning to their local depots brought the regiments up to war strength, and they then set off by train for their concentration areas. The process did not go perfectly, but it was effectively complete just 18 days after the mobilisation order. Including the southern allies and all the reserves and Landwehr, 1,183,000 men had been mobilised (equivalent to the population of a major European city), with everything from food and ammunition to military doctors and lawyers, and 462,000 had been concentrated on the frontier. By the war's end, the Federal – by then Imperial – Army in France numbered 850,000 troops.

By late July no French attack had materialised apart from a few cavalry skirmishes, and the Prussian armies continued the move to their concentration areas: First Army (65,000 men) near Wadern, Second Army (174,000) near Neunkirken, and Third Army (141,000) near Landau. King Wilhelm joined his Royal Headquarters at Mainz on 31 July. Moltke's plan was for Second Army in the centre to advance towards Saarbrücken with First Army moving parallel to its north, and Third Army (which was intended to move first) advancing towards Strasbourg. The expectation was now that the French would meet Second Army's thrust head-on, and that either First Army or Third Army (or both) would then envelop them from the side.

Meanwhile the French mobilisation, which had not been prepared or planned in the Prussian fashion, degenerated into chaos. Regiments were recruited from across France and reservists might live anywhere, meaning that formations would take about a month to reach full strength. But given the urgency of the situation, French plans combined mobilisation with concentration, so that regiments departed for their frontier concentration areas understrength, leaving the rest of their men and equipment to follow. About 2,000 separate contingents, each of 50–300 reservists, gathered together at towns throughout France, travelled first to their regimental depots, and then on to join their regiments. Stories became rife after the war of reservists living almost on the frontier with Germany journeying to their depots in southern France, Algeria or Corsica, and then back to their regiments on the frontier, only to arrive too late. Once more the French Army improvised; in addition to the Garde Mobile being used to augment the line infantry, formations known as *Régiments de Marche* were formed by combining battalions from different units.

The only plan that the French could implement had been drawn up in 1868, creating three armies based on the main rail routes which ran into Metz and Strasbourg. The Army of Alsace assembled at Strasbourg under Marshal MacMahon, the Army of Lorraine at Metz under Marshal Bazaine, and the Army of Châlons (the main military training camp in northern France, north of the town itself) under Marshal François-Antoine Canrobert. This was changed on 11 July, as the war crisis deepened, when Napoleon III decided that he must command in person. There would be only one army, the optimistically named Army of the Rhine, and the three marshals would each command a strong army corps of four divisions within it. Despite the change of name and organisation, the mobilisation plan continued essentially as it was, with seven army corps (three of which were new or improvised formations) strung out from Thionville on the River Moselle to Strasbourg; and Canrobert's command at

The battle of Wissembourg, 4 August 1870. This imaginative French popular print depicts an attack by *Turcos*, North African infantry part of the division of Major General Abel Douay of MacMahon's I Corps. Douay was killed in the battle and his division virtually destroyed. (Ann Ronan Picture Library)

Châlons, now designed VI Corps, forming the reserve. The nature both of the railways and the hilly frontier terrain meant that the Army of the Rhine was in effect divided into two wings, three army corps and the Imperial Guard to the north, and three army corps to the south. By the time that Napoleon arrived at Metz on 28 July to take command, bringing with him both his 14-year-old son, the Prince Imperial, and Marshal Leboeuf as his chief of staff, only 200,000 French soldiers had been mobilised. In the face of inadequate supplies and equipment many troops had to fend for themselves, or wandered around looking for their units.

The Army of the Rhine began to advance on 31 July, but lack of proper staffwork and preparation meant that its army corps became entangled with each other on the country roads; the soldiers were left with little food and shelter, as well as a growing sense of the inadequacy of their leaders.

Only 39,000 reservists had reached their regiments, and the army's total strength (which remains hard to estimate accurately) was at most 280,000 troops, ready to fight for France but ill-equipped and ill-supplied, with a confused organisation, inadequate transport and no agreed plan of campaign.

On 2 August the French II Corps in the centre pushed forward across the frontier to capture Saarbrücken against token resistance, hailed as a great success in Paris. The young Prince Imperial, who came to see the battlefield, was delighted to pick up a spent bullet as a souvenir. But the combination of poor supply and organisation, and general indecision at Napoleon's Imperial Headquarters, left the French vulnerable to the Prussian response. On 5 August the aggressive General von Steinmetz swung his First Army southwards against II Corps at Saarbrücken, and also across the line of advance intended for Second Army in complete violation of Moltke's orders. In response, II Corps pulled back to the Spicheren-Stiering heights above the town to await First Army's attack.

The battle of Spicheren on 6 August set the pattern for a succession of Prussian victories. A French force of 32,000 in strong defences was blundered into by Prussian forces that built up in the course of the day as more units arrived, finally numbering 67,000 troops. The Prussians took heavy casualties, but used their artillery to beat down the French rifle fire, while exploiting their increasing strength and the French inability to move to find and envelop the flanks of the position. By nightfall the French had given way and retreated.

Meanwhile to the south, the Prussian Third Army also began its advance. On 4 August it encountered a weak division of MacMahon's I Corps that had pushed forward to Wissembourg, where it held the town and its old fortress as well as the hills to the south. The Prussians advanced blindly through the difficult and wooded hill country, taking heavy losses from fire, but in the course of the day their 50,000 men outflanked about 5,000 French and drove them back. Next day the reality of the French situation was acknowledged at Imperial Headquarters: MacMahon was given independent command of the three southern army corps including his own, and assembled 45,000 men to defend another wooded ridgeline at Wörth against the 130,000 men and 100 guns of Third Army. The French V Corps, which could have supported MacMahon, held its positions some distance away, both unable and unwilling to move.

The battle of Wörth (or Fröschwiller-Wörth – the French and Germans often gave the same battles different names) was fought on 6 August, the same day as the battle of Spicheren. Prussian and Bavarian artillery overcame French rifle fire, and increasingly desperate French cavalry charges over impossible ground achieved nothing except to buy time for MacMahon's forces to retreat. In disarray and out of contact with the French forces to the north, MacMahon announced his intention to fall back all the way to Châlons to regroup. Napoleon at first confirmed this as a general order for all forces to retire on Châlons, giving up a considerable part of eastern France. But as individual army corps, particularly II Corps

in the centre, were already retiring to Metz, Napoleon instead ordered all but MacMahon's forces to unite there.

So, within a week of the fighting starting two French armies, soon renamed the Army of Metz and the Army of Châlons respectively (although many were unaware of the change), were in full retreat. The shock was felt throughout France and efforts to increase the forces were redoubled. Plans for a Baltic expedition were cancelled, the sailors and marines were hurried to Paris and recruiting of conscripts for the Paris National Guard and for the Garde Mobile throughout France was increased. On 9 August Olliver resigned, and General Cousin de Mantauban the Count de Palikao took over as both premier and minister of war. Refugees from the countryside started to pour into Paris; in the assembly and in the cafés and among the Red revolutionaries there was already talk of a republic.

Within the field armies and among senior French officers also, there was a growing sense that too much loyalty to the Empire might not be advisable. On 7 August the hot weather broke into torrential rain for several days, causing flooding and misery for both sides. Moltke and his staff officers needed to disentangle First Army and Second Army at Saarbrücken, and the main Prussian advance did not resume until 9 August, although cavalry patrols were pushed forward. As the Prussian Third Army followed up the retreating MacMahon, both sides became increasingly separated from the forces to their north by the Vosges mountains. But by 12 August, Third Army was through the passes of the Vosges and had regained contact with Second Army to its north. Of two small French fortresses on the way, Phalsbourg held out until 12 December, and Bitsch, besieged by Bavarian troops, only surrendered on 26 March 1871, long after the fighting elsewhere had ended; other troops from Third Army including the Baden Division turned south to besiege Strasbourg, reaching it on 14 August. Without their supply trains, Moltke's troops had to live off the land by requisition and confiscation.

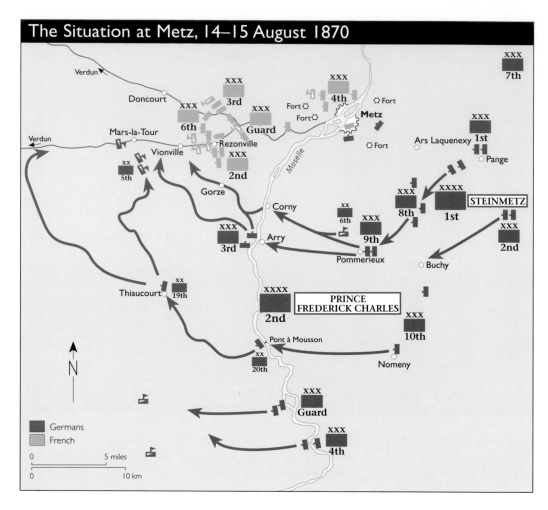

The Situation at Metz, 14–15 August 1870

This problem of fortresses and fortress towns, which acted as supply bases and controlled the rail routes, was soon to become a dominant issue for both sides.

Also on 12 August, Napoleon III handed command of the Army of Metz to Marshal Bazaine and announced his intention to leave for Châlons, to which Bazaine should bring the army after getting it across the Moselle. The three army corps and the Imperial Guard continued to converge on Metz, where Marshal Canrobert had arrived with his VI Corps from Châlons (without most of its artillery and entrenching equipment), just before Prussian cavalry cut the direct railway route. Bazaine's position was a difficult one: Canrobert, who was senior, had declined to take the army command; while Napoleon himself was

reluctant to actually leave, keeping command of the Imperial Guard and issuing informal orders to the other army corps commanders. Temporary bridges across the Moselle were being washed away in the floods and a day was lost in organising the crossing. By the afternoon of 14 August only half the French troops had crossed the river by seven bridges, before threading their way through the twisting streets of the old city and westward to their camping grounds.

Not fully realising the desperate state of their enemy, the Prussians assumed that the French would make a stand on the line of the Moselle. Prussian plans were for Third Army to continue its pursuit of MacMahon, and First Army to push Bazaine back into Metz, while Second Army, pivoting on First Army, advanced between them to cross the

The battle of Mars-la-Tour, 16 August 1870

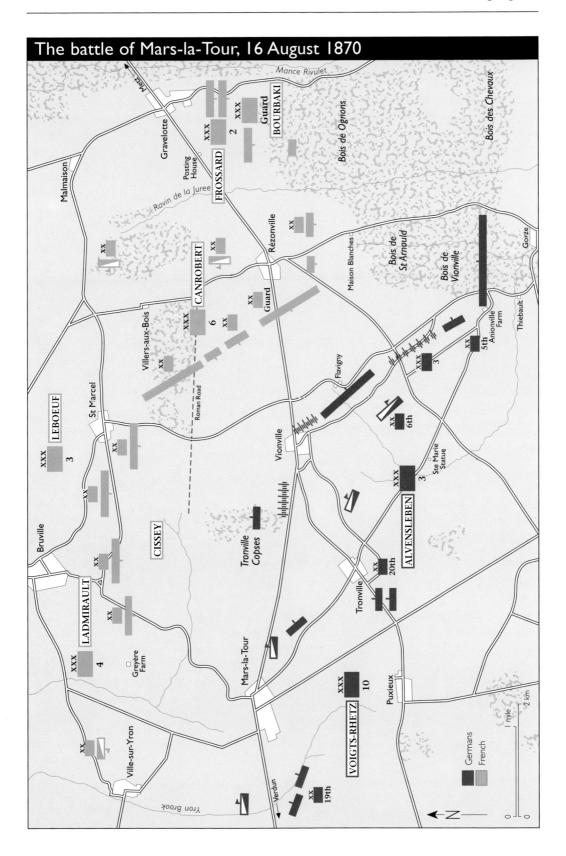

Mance Rivulet

Bois des Chevaux

Bois de Ognons

2 XXX Guard BOURBAKI

XXX 2

Gravelotte

Posting House

Malmaison

FROSSARD

Ravin de la Jurée

Rézonville

XX

Bois de St Arnould

Bois de Vionville

Gorze

Maison Blanches

5th

Anionville Farm

Thiebault

CANROBERT

Guard

XXX 6

XX

XX

XXX 3

Villers-aux-Bois

XX

Roman Road

Flavigny

St Marcel

LEBOEUF

XXX 3

XX

6th XX

Ste Marie Statue

ALVENSLEBEN

XXX 3

Bruville

CISSEY

Vionville

Tronville Copses

20th XX

LADMIRAULT

XX

XX

XXX 4

Greyère Farm

Tronville

Mars-la-Tour

Puxieux

Ville-sur-Yron

XX

VOIGTS-RHETZ

XXX 10

Verdun

Yron Brook

19th XX

N

Germans

French

1 mile

2 km

Moselle south of Metz near Pont-à-Mousson, so pre-empting any attempt by MacMahon to advance northwards and re-unite the French forces. This was seen as a considerable risk by the Prussians, exposing the individual formations of Second Army to a possible French counter-attack as they crossed the river. On the late afternoon of 14 August the leading Prussian VII Corps of First Army attacked the French forces still east of the Moselle in the battle of Borny (also known as Borny-Colombey or Colombey-Nouilly from the chain of villages to the east of Metz), with again other

Prussian forces joining in. The French III Corps took the brunt of the attack, and part of their IV Corps had to recross the Moselle to support it, adding to the French delays.

Both sides claimed Borny as a victory, with more justification in the case of the Prussians. They assumed that, with the direct road to Châlons cut, Bazaine's Army of Metz would retreat as rapidly as possible westward to the next main fortress town of Verdun, about 30 miles (50 km) away. On 15 August Moltke ordered Second Army, after crossing the Meuse, to advance west and then north to get across the Metz–Verdun road, adding

in characteristic style that 'The commander of the Second Army is entrusted with this operation which he will conduct according to his own judgement and with the means at his disposal, that is to say all the Corps of his Army.'

The French plan was indeed to retreat to Verdun, but moving their forces – together with Imperial hangers-on, officers' luxuries, personal baggage and other impediments – over the bridges and through Metz imposed much greater delays than the Prussians expected; in three days they had moved less than 10 miles (16 km). By the evening of

15 August, the day on which the rain finally stopped, their II and VI Corps and the Imperial Guard were encamped west of Metz, while the troops of III and IV Corps were crossing the river and settling down to the north-west. Never expecting the French to be so slow, the Prussian Second Army issued orders based on the assumption that Bazaine's advance guards had almost reached Verdun, and that a swift attack northwards might catch the French in marching columns from the flank.

At dawn on 16 August, a day remembered by French veterans as being 'as hot as Mexico', Napoleon III finally left the Army of Metz for Châlons by train, with orders to Bazaine to follow him via Verdun as rapidly as possible, but on no account to suffer a further defeat. Bazaine had already issued orders that II and VI Corps might be attacked next day. Shortly after Napoleon left, since French cavalry patrols reported no enemy to the south and the last troops of III and IV Corps had still not reached their encampments, Bazaine ordered the march to Verdun delayed until the afternoon. In fact a Prussian cavalry division already lay to the south, the advance guard of their III Corps, and its artillery opened fire on a division of the French II Corps encamped at the village of Vionville shortly after Bazaine had issued his orders.

The battle of Mars-la-Tour (also known variously as the battle of Vionville-Mars-la-Tour and the battle of Rezonville from the villages along the Verdun–Metz road) was a dramatic encounter in which Bazaine's behaviour – like that of Napoleon earlier – almost defied explanation. The commander of the Prussian III Corps, Lieutenant General Konstantin von Alvensleben, assumed at first that he was cutting off the rearguard of a French army that had already marched westwards. Bazaine, with the direct road west

'The Death Ride of Bredow's Brigade at Mars-la-Tour, 16 August 1870'. Troopers of the 7th Magdeburg Cuirassiers ('The White Cuirassiers'), which together with the 16th Altmark Uhlans (and the 13th Dragoons, which did not take part in the charge) formed 12th Cavalry Brigade. Lithograph 1900 by Richard Knoetel (1857–1914). (AKG, Berlin)

The battle of Gravelotte-St Privat, 18 August 1870: The opening moves

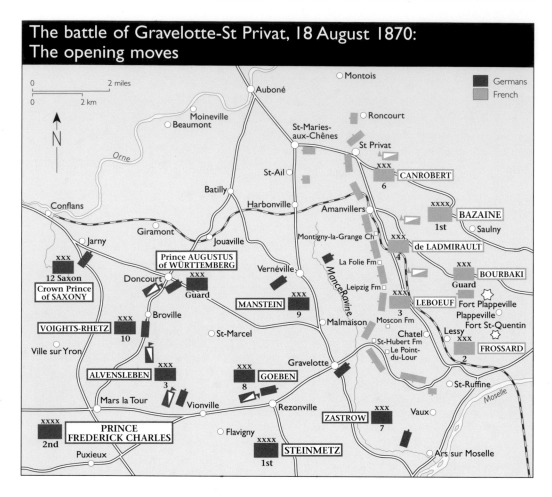

to Verdun blocked, assumed that a major Prussian threat was developing from the south along the line of the Moselle that could cut him off from Metz if it broke through. By midday, as the first troops of the Prussian X Corps also arrived on the battlefield, no more than 30,000 Prussians with their backs to Paris were attacking an entire French army of 135,000 with their backs to the frontier, while away to the south the rest of the Prussian Second Army was marching in the wrong direction.

A Prussian defeat at Mars-la-Tour seemed certain. If Bazaine had swung III and VI Corps south-westwards they would have outflanked and crushed the enemy forces. Instead, although certainly brave and highly active that day, Bazaine gave orders to individual regiments, and at one point was personally caught up in the fighting, but

scarcely issued instructions to his army corps commanders, devoting himself to strengthening his position to the east, where II Corps and the Imperial Guard were well placed to prevent a Prussian breakthrough to Metz. But the simple difference in numbers between the two sides began to wear the Prussians down. With determination and increasing desperation, they launched repeated attacks against the French centre between Vionville and Rezonville, as their only chance of holding the enemy back.

In this war of millions, Mars-la-Tour featured one episode that caught popular imagination and became a military legend, famous throughout Europe and the subject of German paintings, poems and stories: 'The Death Ride'. In the early afternoon, with ammunition running out and reinforcements still some hours away,

The battle of Gravelotte-St Privat, 18 August 1870: The main engagement

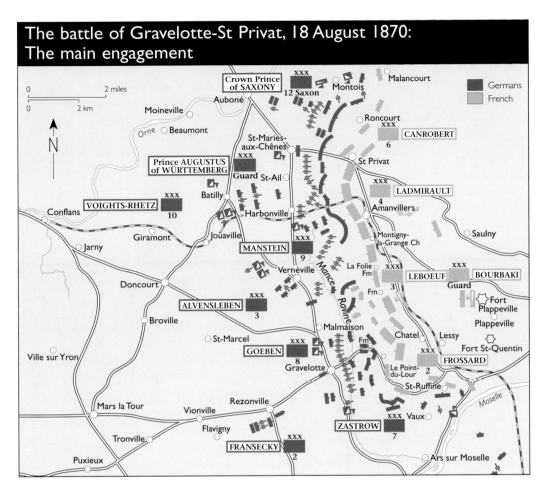

Alvensleben bought time for his beleaguered III Corps by launching a reserve brigade of two heavy cavalry regiments directly at Canrobert's VI Corps in the French centre. (It was Canrobert, watching the Charge of the Light Brigade in the Crimean War, who had famously declared, 'It is magnificent – but it is not war.') Despite heavy losses, the charge achieved its objective in disrupting the French. As more Prussians arrived, the battle also saw the last great charge and mêlée of cavalry divisions against each other in western Europe, near Mars-la-Tour itself. Of Bismarck's sons, Herbert was wounded and Wilhelm's horse was shot from under him; for a while Bismarck believed both were dead. By nightfall the Prussians had 95,000 troops on the battlefield.

Next day, the French pulled back a short distance towards Metz, mainly in order to resupply and rearm, taking up strong positions on ridges running generally south–north from the Moselle to just beyond the village of St Privat, with the Imperial Guard held in reserve. The Prussian Second Army, reinforced to 230,000 men by VII and VIII Corps from First Army, still had no clear idea of the French location or intentions, expecting them either to march north-westwards towards Verdun or to stand and offer battle. Moltke, who had also arrived with Royal Headquarters to direct events, issued orders for 18 August that coped with either possibility: in effect, Second Army would advance pivoting on the Moselle and the village of Gravelotte, with each army corps in turn moving further north and then east. If the French were marching north-west then they would be hit in the flank; if not then the extending Prussian line would outflank the French position and envelop it.

A depiction of Gravelotte-St Privat in a French popular print. This picture gives only the most general impression of the terrain and events of the battle. (Ann Ronan Picture Library)

The battle of Gravelotte-St Privat on 18 August was the first engagement of the war between full-strength field armies on both sides, once more with each combatant facing towards its original base. It broadly followed the Prussian plan, but not as they had intended. The French left wing held by II Corps, closest to the Moselle and to Metz, was extremely strong both in numbers and because of the very difficult ground of the Maunce Ravine in front of the Prussian

advance. Bazaine's headquarters was also behind the left wing at Plappeville, part of the Metz defences, with the Imperial Guard nearby. The French centre was held by III and IV Corps; the right wing at St Privat was in open ground, where the lack of entrenching tools for VI Corps was severely felt. In contrast to his activity at Mars-la-Tour, Bazaine made almost no attempt to issue orders or direct the battle. It was afterwards claimed that his headquarters staff spent most of the day working out awards and promotions for Mars-la-Tour.

As the Prussian advance began, cavalry patrols reported that the French were standing to fight. Moltke again made little

VIII Corps, issued repeated orders for the men to press forward. The result was a series of piecemeal attacks that produced heavy Prussian losses.

To the north, an error in Second Army staffwork sent the Prussian Guard and XII Saxon Corps down the same road simultaneously, delaying the advance of both. In mid-afternoon the Prussian Guard, believing that it had found the French northern flank, launched the first of a series of attacks against St Privat and its surrounding farms and smaller villages in the face of murderous French fire, which again became the subject of epic depictions of heroism. Not even the iron discipline and self-belief of the Guard could overcome the Mitrailleuse and the extra range of the Chassepot rifle over the Dreyse, and the Prussians once more resorted to their artillery. In the early evening, fire from over 200 Prussian guns on St Privat finally caused the French to break, the Prussian Guard took the village, and XII Saxon Corps at last enveloped the French line from the north-west. The fleeing troops of IV and VI Corps ran into the leading division of the Imperial Guard, moving up from reserve into the setting sun to save the situation. General Charles Bourbaki, commanding the Imperial Guard, refused to continue his advance, complaining that 'you promised me victory, now you get me involved in a rout!' and the sight of the Guard retreating was enough to cause a general French collapse.

By nightfall the French had retired within the ring of forts that defended Metz, and the Prussians – on both sides of the Moselle – had them surrounded. In both armies, the morale of many individual soldiers remained high, and despite their flight the French were quite prepared to fight on. Men of Canrobert's VI Corps cheered him at the end of the battle, and the epic of St Privat was remembered as a brave and heroic defence by French soldiers let down by Bazaine. The battle had, in fact, been a close one. The battalions of the Prussian Guard involved in the attack on St Privat lost about half their number and the total Prussian losses were

effort to control events, trusting to skill and training. The battle commenced just before midday with an exchange of artillery fire that lasted the rest of the afternoon. The Prussian commanders, taught to attack and seek battle almost regardless, launched their men directly at the first French that they encountered, and came close to smashing their own army to pieces against the French positions. The Prussian IX Corps became engaged first, with troops of VII and VIII Corps joining in to the south, trying to make headway through the difficult terrain against the strongest part of the French line. General von Steinmetz, although his First Army no longer actually commanded

ABOVE The cemetery at St Privat during the battle.
A painting by Alphonse de Neuville (1835–85).
(Ann Ronan Picture Library)

BELOW 'King Wilhelm on the Battlefield at Metz.'
The king with his troops at the end of the battle of
Gravelotte-St Privat. Lithograph, 1871. (AKG, Berlin)

heavy – over 20,000 casualties to the French 12,000 (including almost 4,500 French taken prisoners) – the inevitable product of their bludgeoning style of warfare. It was the largest and also the bloodiest battle of the war, with losses that shocked King Wilhelm.

Trapping the best army that France possessed in the fortress of Metz was a major Prussian victory, the culmination of the single continuous operation that had begun with Moltke's order for mobilisation on 16 July; but it was not the end of the war. On 19 August, Moltke issued orders for the next phase of operations. First Army and part of Second Army would remain to besiege Metz, about 170,000 men in an encirclement of 30 miles (50 km) under the overall command of Prince Frederick Charles (the insubordinate General von Steinmetz was removed from commanding First Army on 15 September to become governor of Posen – modern Posnan). From the remainder of Second Army, Moltke created a new Fourth Army – known as the Army of the Meuse and numbering 86,000 troops – under Crown Prince Albert of Saxony, made up of his own XII Saxon Corps, IV Corps and the Prussian Guard. In contrast to the French organisational problems, the Prussians under their new army command arrangements were ready to continue next day. The Army of the Meuse advanced westward in co-operation with Third Army, which had halted its advance near Toul while the battles west of Metz took place and was now ordered to continue onward towards Châlons.

At their camp at Châlons, the retreating French troops from I Corps, V Corps and VII Corps constituted the remainder of France's effective field army, together with the newly-formed XII Corps (one improvised division, one of sailors and marines, and one of untrained new arrivals) and two cavalry divisions: 120,000 men with 500 guns and Mitrailleuses. As an indication of future problems, attempts to include the Paris area Garde Mobile in the Army of Châlons resulted in so many mutinies that most were allowed to return home.

At a council of war on 17 August, Napoleon III was incapable of making a decision,

saying that 'I seem to have abdicated' and relinquishing all responsibility. With contradictory advice and orders, coming mainly from Empress Eugénie in Paris and from General Palikao as minister of war, no choice open to Marshal MacMahon was very attractive. The state of his army's morale, supplies and organisation all suggested halting at Châlons, but this invited waiting to be attacked, and defeat in yet another envelopment as the Prussian Third Army and the Army of the Meuse approached. To fall back and defend Paris was in military terms the safe move, but politically it would send another signal of French defeat, and might precipitate a revolution. Instead, the commander of XII Corps, General Jules-Louis Trochu, a politically active Catholic and Orléanist who had been an outspoken critic of the French Army's lack of readiness before the war, was made military governor of Paris, and sent to prepare its defence. There remained the hope of MacMahon reaching Metz and joining Bazaine, and nothing less seemed likely to save the Second Empire or France itself; public opinion demanded it.

The resulting decision was a compromise: on 21 August the Army of Châlons left its encampment moving north-westwards towards Rheims, out of the path of a possible encirclement by the two advancing Prussian armies, while remaining between them and Paris, and also on a straight line eastward to Verdun and Metz. Many officers and men were untrained as well as unequipped for war; and the army was so unprepared for its march that substantial stores of clothing and food had to be burnt on departure, while some soldiers lacked shoes and proper uniforms. Despite assurances given to MacMahon, the supplies waiting for him at Rheims proved inadequate, or could not be distributed. Messages sent by Bazaine suggested that he would co-operate with an advance by MacMahon by breaking out of Metz north-westward towards Montmédy, another fortress town close to the Belgian frontier.

So the Army of Châlons left Rheims on 23 August heading north-east, replenishing itself as best it could by foraging and from railway stocks that required a halt at Rethel on the River Aisne. Since the Prussian Army of the Meuse now blocked the direct route through to Verdun, MacMahon continued north-eastwards on 26 August towards Montmédy. As the march resumed, once more the summer rain came down in torrents.

Unknown to MacMahon while he was attempting to reach Metz, Bazaine mounted two assaults on the Prussian line surrounding him in an attempt to break out. The first, aimed towards the north-east on 27 August, was cancelled due to the pouring rain and utter confusion among the assaulting troops. The second attempt, aimed towards the east in the belief that this would surprise the Prussians, began on 31 August and continued next day without breaking through. Known as the battle of Noisseville from the nearest village, it cost over 3,500 French and 2,500 Prussian casualties.

Moltke and his staff were unaware of MacMahon's movements until 24 August, and then could not quite believe that MacMahon was taking his army on a flank march across the front of two of their armies so close to the Belgian frontier, while leaving Paris undefended. Confirmation of MacMahon's advance came next day, partly from Paris newspapers. The Prussian Third Army had crossed the River Meuse on 20 August and continued on towards Châlons, which its leading troops reached on 24 August, with the Army of the Meuse to its north-east. In response to Moltke's orders, both Prussian armies now began to swing north-west and then northward, including marches through the difficult Argonne forest, starting their envelopment of the Army of Châlons wherever they might find it. Next day MacMahon's troops resumed their march eastward, but on 26 August their cavalry patrols made contact with the northernmost of the Prussian forces (actually XII Saxon Corps) advancing almost in the opposite direction, a few miles to the south-east. The French turned two army corps southwards and halted in case of an attack that never came, losing a day's march in the process.

By 28 August the Army of Châlons had entered the wooded hill country at the southern edge of the Ardennes forest region stretching northwards well into Belgium, but had not yet reached the Meuse; while on the Prussian side the Army of the Meuse had completed its great wheel northwards and was closing rapidly from the south, with Third Army a day's march behind to the south-west. For Moltke and his staff it was an affair of marching tables and mathematical calculations; for his troops a hard slog on short rations through blind country; superior Prussian cavalry patrolling was critical in locating the French and harassing their movements. While General Palikao in Paris continued to demand an advance eastward from MacMahon to relieve Bazaine, XII Saxon Corps pushed far enough northwards to cut the bridges across the Meuse, blocking the way to Montmédy. Lacking a pontoon bridging train, and increasingly aware of the threat from the south, MacMahon also learned that Prussian cavalry had arrived at Rheims behind him.

The Prussians still expected MacMahon to stand and fight, with his four weakened army corps against their six strong ones. As efforts to find a way across the Meuse further north continued, exhaustion and despondency took their toll on MacMahon's troops and their commanders. Orders went astray, and soldiers had to march and countermarch over bad dirt roads through the forests and hills, sometimes at night, harassed by Prussian cavalry. The Army of Châlons began to fall apart, retreating north-westwards towards the town of Sedan, lying in the Meuse valley surrounded by hills barely seven miles (11 km) from the Belgian frontier.

In a series of confused encounters among the hills and trees, on 29 August troops of the French V Corps were caught by XII Saxon Corps at the village of Nouart, and then again next day by both I Bavarian Corps and IV Corps at the village of Beaumont on the Meuse south of Sedan, just escaping across the river as XII Saxon Corps joined in once more. The Bavarians also caught and destroyed part of VII Corps on the march close to the same village. MacMahon ordered a general retreat to

Sedan, and many French troops fled through the night and the next morning as best they could, to reach the town in a state of utter exhaustion.

It might still have been possible for the Army of Châlons to escape westwards at once, and MacMahon was much criticised for taking no action, as well as for earlier continuing to obey Palikao's orders from Paris when he knew that they made no sense. Given the state of his troops he ordered a rest day for recovery, apparently expecting the Prussians to halt or attempt a siege, which would still give his Army time to escape. As the Prussians came up in pursuit on 31 August, their XI Corps seized crossings over the Meuse at the village of Donchery to the west of Sedan, and I Bavarian Corps seized crossings to the east at the village of Bazeilles; IV Corps and XII Saxon Corps were set to cross further east still at the village of Douzy before joining the Prussian Guard advancing westwards on the northern side of the river; meanwhile II Bavarian Corps guarded the remaining crossings of the Meuse from the south. Bismarck issued diplomatic warnings to the Belgians that any French soldiers attempting to escape across the frontier must be disarmed, or the Prussians claimed the right to pursue them. 'We have them in a mouse-trap,' exclaimed Moltke on his arrival with Royal Headquarters. One French general was less delicate, comparing their position to 'a chamber-pot'.

The battle of Sedan on 1 September, unlike Gravelotte-St Privat, was a foregone conclusion: numbers, firepower and morale were all on the Prussian side. Two Prussian armies, totalling 224,000 troops, attacked a demoralised, disorganised and exhausted French army half their size. Nevertheless, the French once again made a hard fight of it, holding strong positions with I and XII Corps facing east, VII Corps facing west and north, and the battered V Corps held in reserve; and once again Moltke did not so much direct the attack as fail to restrain his army corps commanders.

At dawn, in the early mist that later gave way to bright sunshine, I Bavarian Corps came over its bridges at Bazeilles and attacked

XII Corps, driving it out of the burning village. In the firefight, there were conflicting claims that the Bavarians had massacred French civilians at Bazeilles or that the French had armed civilians contrary to the laws of war – once more a sign of the future. As XII Saxon Corps arrived in the course of the morning, with IV Corps behind it, the French were driven back into Sedan. At the same time, the Prussian XI Corps crossed the river at Donchery and moved forward, with V Corps behind it coming round to the north to seal off the Belgian frontier, linking hands with the Prussian Guard coming up from the east.

MacMahon had given his army no particular orders for 1 September, apparently expecting another rest day. Riding forward to the fight at Bazeilles, he was wounded and carried back to Sedan, relinquishing command to General Auguste Ducrot of I Corps, who at once ordered a retreat and breakout westward. These orders were immediately countermanded by General Emmanuel Wimpffen, recently arrived from Paris with instructions from Palikao to take command of V Corps and to succeed MacMahon if necessary. The resulting argument between the French generals added to the confusion, but made little difference to the battle's outcome. By midday the Army of Châlons was trapped in Sedan with the Prussians on the heights all around.

The Prussians (and Bavarians and Saxons) had no need to send their infantry forward. Instead they brought up their massed artillery of nearly 500 guns which fired into the town and French positions. King Wilhelm watched the battle from a rise near the village of Frenois just south of the river, accompanied by Bismarck, Moltke, Roon, and the crowd of dignitaries and functionaries with Royal Headquarters. On the other side the Emperor Napoleon, who was almost in a state of collapse from bladder pain, rode from one unit to another, apparently seeking death in battle. Under the weight of Prussian artillery the French gave way in each critical village: Illy on the dominating heights to the north fell early in the afternoon, followed by Floing to the west.

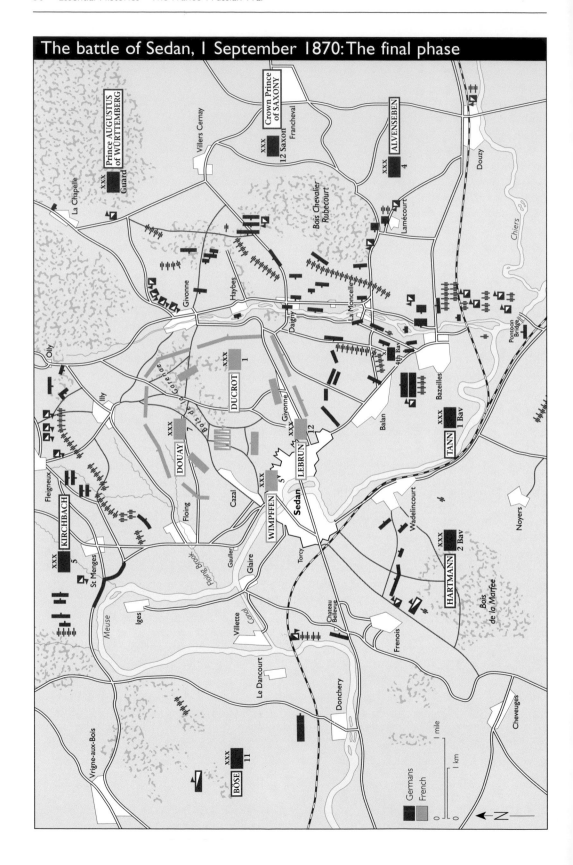

The battle of Sedan, 1 September 1870: The final phase

Prince AUGUSTUS of WÜRTTEMBERG
Guard
xxx

Crown Prince of SAXONY
Francheval
xxx
12 Saxon

ALVENSEBEN
xxx
4

La Chapelle

Villers Cernay

Lamécourt

Douzy

Chiers

Bois Chevalier
Rubécourt

Givonne

Haybes

La Moncelle

Daigny

Olly

Pontoon
Bridge

DUCROT
xxx
1

4th Bav

Illy

Bazeilles

Bois de Garenne

DOUAY
xxx
7

Givonne

LEBRUN
xxx
12

Balan

TANN
xxx
1 Bav

Fleigneux

Floing

Cazal

WIMPFEN
xxx
5

Sedan

KIRCHBACH
xxx
5

St Menges

Gaulier

Glaire

Torcy

Wadelincourt

Noyers

HARTMANN
xxx
2 Bav

Floing Brook

Iges

Meuse

Villette

Chateau
Bellevue

Frenois

Bois
de la Marfée

Le Dancourt

Doncheery

Cheveuges

Vrigne-aux-Bois

BÖSE
xxx
11

1 mile

1 km

Germans
French

N

In desperation, the French launched their remaining cavalry division in repeated charges against the Prussians at Floing, attempting to clear a path for the rest of their forces to escape. Each time the Prussian line held firm, the French re-formed and charged again, suffering heavy losses with each charge. 'Ah! Those brave men!' King Wilhelm wondered. A story spread that the last few survivors, coming forward to charge again, were saluted by the Prussian infantry who let them pass by to safety.

Within a few hours French resistance began to cease. Troops sought refuge from the shelling in woods or buildings, some trying to get into the medieval citadel of Sedan itself, the gates of which were barred against them. In the wood of Garenne north of the town white flags were hoisted, soon followed by others. At about 5.00 pm, Napoleon himself demanded that the fighting should stop and the enemy should be asked for an armistice. The idea of surrender was still too much for some French troops: in the 'battle of the last cartridges' more than 1,000 of them stormed into the village of Balan, briefly driving the Bavarians back, but could get no further. A white flag was flown above the citadel and Moltke sent a representative forward to discover its significance. He returned with a message for King Wilhelm: 'Having been unable to die in

The battle of Sedan, 1 September 1870. An imaginative depiction of a stampede of French troops through the town in an attempt to escape the Prussian onslaught. Wood engraving from *The Graphic*, 24 September 1870. (Ann Ronan Picture Library)

the midst of my troops, there remains nothing for me but to deliver my sword into Your Majesty's hands. I am Your Majesty's true brother, Napoleon'.

The events of the next day were repeatedly depicted with varying accuracy in

A French popular print showing the surrender of Napoleon III at Sedan on 2 September 1870. Although the Emperor, being desperately ill, did travel by carriage with a Prussian cavalry escort to meet Bismarck, this print depicts a republican legend that he was comfortably unconcerned and smoking a cigar, while French soldiers turned their backs on him in disgust. (Ann Ronan Picture Library)

paintings and writings. After a brief interview with Bismarck, Napoleon III signed the capitulation at 11.00 am on 2 September. Of 124,000 troops with the Army of Châlons at Sedan, 17,000 were killed or wounded and 21,000 taken prisoner in the battle while a further 83,000 surrendered under the terms agreed; only 3,000 escaped to be disarmed in Belgium; Napoleon was taken to be a prisoner in Prussia. With Bazaine and his troops still besieged in Metz, France no longer had an effective army in the field.

The news broke in Paris next day, and on Sunday 4 September a determined mob

including soldiers of the Paris National Guard overthrew the Assembly. The Empress Eugénie fled and the Third Republic was proclaimed. General Trochu became president of a Government of National Defence, with the moderate Republican Jules Favre as vice-president, and the radical Léon Gambetta (of Italian-Jewish ancestry) as minister for the interior. In fact Napoleon had not abdicated, and he had made clear to Bismarck that his surrender was personal, not made in the name of France. On 6 September an official proclamation announced that the Government of National Defence wanted peace, but refused to concede any territory or people to the Prussians: 'Not an inch of our soil, or a stone of our fortresses, will we cede.'

As soon as the Army of Châlons had surrendered at Sedan, Moltke gave orders for Third Army and the Army of the Meuse to prepare to march towards Paris with 150,000 troops, moving off five days later. As the Prussians approached, General Trochu and his government increased preparations for the city's defence. Within the ring of 16 forts that defended Paris were a division of sailors and marines, about 100,000 Garde Mobile, and up to 350,000 members of the Paris National Guard, which was a focus of political discontent rather than a force capable of fighting the Prussian Army. About 60,000 soldiers of the new French XIII Corps (which had been meant to join MacMahon) and XIV Corps were rushed to Paris, in varying states of preparedness. Sheep and cattle for food were herded into the city centre; trees were chopped down to provide fuel and barricades. Part of the Government of National Defence was relocated as a precaution to Tours, the next major town south-west of Orléans in the valley of the River Loire, although the leading government members including Trochu all stayed in Paris.

The first Prussian forces reached the outskirts of Paris on 17 September, with the Army of the Meuse moving round to the north and Third Army round to the south. The first battle fought by the republic took place on 19 September as an ill-organised force of 28,000 soldiers including Garde Mobile troops attacked out of Paris against the Prussian southern wing at Chatillon, only to break and recoil. Next day the Prussian encirclement of Paris, in what they called their 'Iron Ring', was completed. King Wilhelm's Royal Headquarters established itself at the palace of Versailles to the west of the city.

For the rest of the century, the Franco-Prussian War would be remembered and studied in terms of this remarkable series of operations by the Army of the North German Confederation against the Second Empire: the battles leading to the trapping of

Ghost of Louis XIV (*to Ghost of Napoleon I*): '*Is this the end of "All the Glories?"*' A cartoon by John Tenniel from *Punch*, 15 October 1870. The ghosts of Napoleon I and King Louis XIV (the 'Sun King') lament that their palace of Versailles is now the headquarters of King Wilhelm I of Prussia, who sits surveying a map of Paris. (Ann Ronan Picture Library)

Bazaine's army in Metz, the surrender of Napoleon III with the Army of Châlons at Sedan, and the investment of Paris. It had taken just over seven weeks, and for the Prussians this was another 'seven weeks war', as in 1866. The main Prussian forces were divided between the investment of Metz by First Army and Second Army, and the investment of Paris by Third Army and the Army of the Meuse. The rest of the army, including Landwehr divisions and other reserve forces, was largely occupied blockading various French fortified towns and cities. The fortress town of Toul fell to bombardment on 25 September, opening a main railway line through to the Prussians at Paris, but the siege of Strasbourg alone continued to occupy 40,000 troops. The new Prussian XIII Corps had to be used to protect the lines of communication between Metz and Strasbourg, with a further XIV Corps being organised later.

There was neither the political desire from Bismarck nor the military need for Moltke to do more. Without an army the Third Republic had no way to make war. For the new French government to do anything but make peace on Prussia's terms was futile – indeed, from the Prussian point of view it was irresponsible.

The Prussian strategy of a shock defeat followed by a peace treaty and acceptance of inferior status had succeeded with the Austrian Empire in 1866, in what had been portrayed largely as a quarrel among Germans. But now the same behaviour was being expected of the strongest, proudest and most self-aware nation in Europe. Particularly in Paris, with the change of government there was a new mood. Representatives of other countries noted this, and were prepared to await developments rather than demanding peace; indeed the speed of the Prussian victory had once more stunned Europe.

The Second Empire had picked a fight with Prussia over an apparently trivial matter and had been humiliated, but the Third Republic had not yet had its chance to fight. In a similar way, many French soldiers felt that they had fought hard and bravely, but had been betrayed by an emperor who had led them to defeat. The Army of Châlons, after all, had been no worse trained and equipped than many armies with which Napoleon I had won great victories. In contrast to attitudes on the war's outbreak, there was considerable popular support throughout France for its continuation. The traditions of the republic in 1793 were revived, as orators called on patriotic citizens to demand their chance to defend their country. Prussia could believe that the war was over, but France was not yet ready to make peace.

Captain Léonce Patry

Several senior officers on both sides wrote their memoirs, usually in self-justification, particularly in the case of Marshal Bazaine. Moltke's chief of intelligence, Lieutenant Colonel Julius von Verdy de Vernois, complained in his memoirs of the stupidity of French peasants in fleeing from Prussian troops: 'All this kind of destruction would be avoided, and the necessary requisitions carried out in a more orderly manner, if the inhabitants remained at home.' Some ordinary soldiers told of their experiences, including Bavarians disturbed by their own behaviour at Bazeilles and later. One wrote of the winter campaign in the Loire valley: 'Through sickness our ranks dwindled in an alarming manner, and it was no rarity for 15, even 20 men from a company to be left behind because of exhaustion, who would then drag themselves along on a wagon or on foot at night.' Many on both sides had fought in previous wars: the Prussians in 1864 and 1866, the French in the Crimea, in Italy and in Mexico. Sadly, the French Colonel Charles Ardent du Picq, whose highly influential writings on the Franco-Austrian War began the serious study of ordinary troops in warfare, was killed by shellfire outside Metz on 15 August.

There are also valuable perspectives from soldiers of other countries. The young Lieutenant Herbert Kitchener of the British Army served as a volunteer with a French medical unit at the battle of Le Mans. This experience of using untrained troops in battle still coloured his attitudes as Field Marshal Lord Kitchener at the start of the First World War. A number of United States officers who were veterans of the Civil War also came to France, mostly viewing events from a perspective of highly critical superiority, including Major General Philip Sheridan, who generally felt that Prussian brutality towards the French did not go far enough.

Given the outcome of the war, its experiences may be represented through the recollections of two junior officers: a Prussian who became famous, and a Frenchman whose career ended in failure.

Captain Paul Ludwig Hans von Beneckendorff und von Hindenburg was a model of a Prussian officer. On the outbreak of the war, Hindenburg was 23 years old, serving as adjutant of the 1st Battalion of the Prussian 3rd Regiment of Foot Guards. From an East Prussian Junker family with a military tradition going back centuries, Hindenburg's father was an army officer, his mother the daughter of another, and he went automatically to officer cadet school. He was unconcerned with the political causes of wars, loyal only to his king, his country, his God, his family, and not least to the Prussian Army. He had fought in the Austro-Prussian War, been wounded at Königgrätz, and decorated for bravery. In the Franco-Prussian War, Hindenburg's regiment formed part of the Prussian Guard Corps, originally in First Army.

Captain von Hindenburg took part in the battle of Gravelotte-St Privat, including the assault on St Privat village itself, in which his regiment suffered 1,096 casualties. After the battle he became adjutant at regimental headquarters. His regiment was held in reserve at Sedan on 1 September, where Hindenburg was an observer. It reached the outskirts of Paris on 19 September and took its place in the encircling siege lines. In January 1871 Hindenburg was sent with a sergeant as his regiment's representative to the ceremony in the Hall of Mirrors at Versailles to witness the proclamation of the new Emperor Wilhelm I of Germany. After the armistice he visited Paris itself, recording his disdainful impressions of the French temperament as 'too vivacious, and therefore too capricious for my taste'. Like others in the new German Army, Hindenburg (who continued to think of himself as a Prussian) was an observer from a distance of the suppression of the Commune in May, before returning with his regiment to Prussia to take part in a triumphal march through Berlin.

Retiring from the army as a general in 1911, Hindenburg returned to active service in 1914, and went on to become a field marshal and in 1916–18 Chief of the Great General Staff, effectively warlord of Germany. After the First World War, Hindenburg, as a symbol to many Germans of their country's former greatness, became involved in right-wing politics. He was president of the new Germany from 1925 until his death in 1934, playing a part in the rise of Adolf Hitler.

Marie Gabriel Léonce Patry, who also wrote his memoirs of the war, experienced some of the same episodes as Hindenburg. Born in Paris of Norman origins and 29 when the war began, he was the son of a schoolmaster who had obtained a free place for him at the officer training academy at Saint-Cyr on hardship grounds. Promoted to lieutenant in 1867, he served in the 1st Battalion of the 6th Infantry Regiment of the Line. In July 1870 he was at the regimental depot at Charleville, while the regiment was garrisoned some distance away at Mézières. Disregarding orders to report to Saint-Cyr as an instructor, Patry was determined to fight, and managed to be put in charge of 300 reservists assembling at Mézières to rejoin the regiment, which had already departed by train for Lorraine. Throughout the war, he kept a notebook that became the basis of his later memoirs.

On 29 July Patry and his men disembarked at the railhead at Thionville, north of Metz, but were unable to find their regiment. Joining other troops marching eastwards, they reached the regiment next day, forming part of IV Corps. Patry actually crossed over the frontier into the Palatinate, near Ittersdorf

west of Saarlouis, on 2 August, before taking part in the retreat to Metz with his regiment, reaching the eastern outskirts of the city on 13 August. Typical of French mobilisation problems was that on this date his regiment numbered 1,807 compared to its notional full strength of more than 2,400 men. Patry's account is a litany of complaints, poor staffwork, poor food, and marching weather that was either hot and dusty, or too much

A highly imaginative depiction of hand-to-hand fighting during the battle of St Quentin, 19 January 1871, from a wood engraving, c.1880. It was this sort of romantic depiction of battle of which Léonce Patry was so critical in his memoirs. (Ann Ronan Picture Library)

rain. He is particularly critical of the captain commanding his company, whom he depicts as a coward and a fool.

Patry was under fire for the first time on 14 August at the battle of Borny. His regiment was hardly involved in the battle of Mars-la-Tour, of which he recorded only his own confused impressions. 'I heard the episode narrated in five or six different ways', he wrote of one general's death in action. 'I became certain that most of the great feats so preciously reported by history were nearly always invented.' Two days later at the battle of Gravelotte-St Privat, Patry's regiment was heavily engaged just south of St Privat itself, probably close enough to see

Captain von Hindenburg's battalion. Patry describes the strain of being under fire in his third battle in five days. 'Was it bad morale?' he wonders. 'When we were lying in the furrow, inactive and impotent under that hellish fire which tried us without our being able to return blow for blow, I was overtaken by a strong desire to be elsewhere; not, however, at the regimental depot.' Patry's company eventually broke and ran from the battlefield, an experience that he shared without understanding it or remembering much about it, and he ended up with the rest of the army trapped in the siege of Metz.

Patry's account of being besieged at Metz includes a bayonet charge by his own

battalion on 31 August, and his increasing contempt for all staff officers. While trapped at Metz he was promoted to captain on 15 September, which gave him great satisfaction, and made battalion adjutant. Two days later he heard Bazaine's proclamation that the emperor was a prisoner and the republic had been formed, news that he says most of the troops received with indifference. On 27 October, when Bazaine surrendered at Metz, Patry records that 'the political aspect, which had to some extent passed me by, suddenly appeared to me in all its sordid reality.' He and other officers, rather than become prisoners in Germany, chose to dress in civilian clothes and escape to continue the fight. Travelling by cart with the aid of local people, on 6 November Patry and his friends crossed the border into neutral Luxemburg, where the customs guards willingly let them through, then took a train to Brussels, and by 10 November he was back in France at Lille.

Captain Patry was given command of a company improvised from troops of the 75th Infantry Regiment of the Line. Travelling with his men by train to Albert (near Amiens, later famous in the First World War as a British base), he joined his battalion as part of the Army of the North under General Bourbaki, later replaced by General Louis Faidherbe. Campaigning in winter in the Somme region, Patry's chief concerns became how his inexperienced troops would cope in battle, and once more the problems of staffwork and the weather. In late December the Army of the North was reorganised, and Patry's battalion became 2nd Battalion of the 67th Régiment de Marche (made up from two battalions of the 75th and one battalion of the 65th Infantry Regiment of the Line). Patry records that he was offered the post of divisional chief of staff with the rank of major, but that he declined, preferring to command fighting troops.

On 23 December Patry and his men took a minor part in the battle of Pont-Noyelles – 'their morale was very good, and I was optimistic after this first trial' – and they were also under fire in the battle of Bapaume on 3 January 1871. But in the battle of St Quentin on 19 January 'the men lost their heads' and fled from the battlefield. Patry cynically records that he called out, 'So is there no one who will have the courage to die here doing his duty?' and that the utter failure of 'this piece of arch-pomposity' led him to 'profound scepticism on the subject of the effect that the words spoken by a leader can have on thirty or forty thousand men in perilous circumstances'.

After the armistice, Patry's regiment was sent to Dunkirk where he was surprised to be treated as a hero, then in February by ship to Cherbourg. When peace was announced the regiment moved by train to Paris. With Patry temporarily in command of his battalion, the regiment entered the city centre on 9 March and camped in the Luxemburg Gardens, where he listened to the 'foolish nonsense' of other people's war stories. With the uprising of the Commune on 18 March, the regiment was ordered out of the city to Versailles, and then returned in April to take part in the siege and the Commune's suppression. Understandably, Patry writes that 'this campaign deeply repelled me', partly because he considered that it was drawn out longer than necessary for political reasons. His own company, now down to 75 men, took seven casualties fighting the Communards.

Patry was decorated for his actions with the Army of the North, but says that he refused a second decoration for helping suppress the Commune. He married in 1872 and rose to lieutenant colonel by 1884. Three years later, when 46 years old, a financial scandal forced him to leave the army. In 1896, cleared of all debt, he was made chief of staff of a reserve division. A year later he published his memoirs of the Franco-Prussian War, written largely from the conviction that no-one understood the war as he had experienced it. He retired from the reserve in 1914 at the age of 72, managed to return to duty for the First World War, retired again from ill-health in 1915, and died in 1917.

The people's war

In September 1870 the new French Government of National Defence had only a limited mandate for its actions. The provinces of France accepted changes of government from Paris, but since 1830, given the chance in plebiscites or elections, they had voted for Monarchists or Bonapartists in preference to Republicans. But Prussia needed a stable French government with which to reach a peace settlement, and the Third Republic was the only realistic choice. On 18 September, as Moltke's troops surrounded Paris, Bismarck gave Vice-President Favre the same terms that he had offered Napoleon on 2 September: France must surrender Strasbourg and Metz, and with them the surrounding territory of Alsace and part of Lorraine. The Prussian demand was prompted partly by traditional power politics and the need for the two fortress towns for military security, but also by pressure from southern German liberals and from newspapers that the Germans of Alsace and Lorraine must be liberated. Favre told Bismarck that 'you want to destroy France', and left in tears.

Members of the French government and others now called for a *guerre à l'outrance* (war without restraint, or total war) against the Prussians. The victorious Prussians assumed that defeated France would pay for their war by an indemnity, and that France did not have the resources to continue fighting. But critically for this stage of the war, Prussia had no effective navy. French maritime trade and commerce were largely unaffected by the end of the Second Empire, and so was French credit overseas; the French economy did not collapse, and the war continued to be financed, in part by borrowing on foreign money markets. French troops were brought back from

garrisons overseas and weapons shipped in from other countries. Factories outside the Prussian zone of occupation also continued to produce weapons, uniforms and equipment.

Wars in 19th century Europe were increasingly about cities as centres of population and industrial production, but were still fought largely in the countryside; literally, on 'campaign'. Most French people

A patrol of Prussian Uhlans galloping through the French countryside, in this case chasing one of the manned balloons escaping from the siege of Paris. Woodcut, 1881. (Ann Ronan Picture Library)

lived as rural peasants in small, stable village communities, indifferent to the outside world, including Paris. Educated Prussians were surprised that many peasants spoke in a local patois or dialect rather than Parisian French. As the forces of either side approached, villagers had the choice of running away or of staying in an attempt to appease the arriving soldiers and limit the damage. The arrival even of French troops in 1870 could be a traumatic event. One general described his method of reconnaissance as consisting of seizing a local peasant and telling him, 'you are going to take us to such-and-such a place and we'll give you a glass of [spirits] and a pretty coin' but 'if you take the wrong road you're looking at two men who will blow your head off with pistols'. French soldiers were also more likely to live off the land through requisitions and looting than their enemies.

When the Prussian invasion began, refugees brought stories of swaggering and arrogant Prussians demanding information, billeting in houses and more, or of fearsome Uhlans sweeping through the countryside (*Uhlan* was strictly the German word for lancer, but was applied to all their cavalry). Old people remembered their childhood when in 1814–15 the Uhlans had led the advance of the Prussian Army under Prince Blücher across France. The impact of these invaders on the ordered, inward-looking village communities stamped the identity of 'Prussian' as a term of abuse on the war and on all German soldiers.

The Prussian image of themselves was as sober, pious and industrious, compared to the dissolute French. In Prussia and other German states, most people had also been born in small villages: two-thirds of the adult male population of Berlin in 1870 came originally from outside the city. The victories over Napoleon III made Bismarck and the Prussian Army even more popular than in 1866. But as the war continued, the dead and wounded began to arrive back home, and more men were recalled to the Landwehr, including for service in France. War weariness certainly increased, but the

overwhelming reaction from civilians was to blame the French. The cultural hostility between the two sides extended far beyond the attitudes of those in uniform, and German public opinion sometimes demanded more than even Bismarck wanted.

From the first campaigns of August, the Prussians came under attack along their line of march from *franc-tireurs* ('free shooters' or freedom fighters), armed local forces wearing any uniform or none, and belonging to every possible political or quasi-military organisation. There was not a single day of the war in which fighting did not take place somewhere in France. In addition to this largely spontaneous reaction from the villages, other *franc-tireurs* came from outside the occupied region as volunteers. One notorious group dressed as the 17th century 'Musketeers' made famous by Alexander Dumas' novel. The legendary revolutionary Giuseppe Garibaldi came from Italy to offer himself and a band of followers to fight alongside the republic. Orthodox French officials were alarmed to see women in officers' uniform among Garibaldi's forces, and the badge of the 'International' (the International Workers Association, founded in London in 1864 with Karl Marx as a prominent member, sometimes known as the 'First International'); but Garibaldi was given a command in eastern France, being credited later as the only 'French' general who never suffered a defeat in the war.

The immediate Prussian response to *franc-tireur* warfare was to hang or shoot suspects, usually without even a military trial, and to burn local villages; some of those taken alive were sentenced to hard labour as criminals. Moltke and most of his officers were disgusted by the French government's use of *franc-tireurs* and of untrained Garde Mobile troops. To the Demigods of the Prussian General Staff, the French behaviour was the exact equivalent of a heresy: People's War was the very thing that organised armies existed to prevent happening between civilised European countries. From the narrow perspective of Prussian military professionalism the French action was barbaric, and not least towards their own men: pitting untrained conscripts and armed civilians against the Prussian Army was no better than murder.

The French view was as complex and multi-faceted as the politics of the Third Republic, but the unifying theme was that they were fighting for France, or what they believed France to be. The symbolism of continued struggle and defiance was itself a reaffirmation of France as a nation. Some, including Garibaldi, were 'making war on war', fighting for a vision of eternal peace in a united European republic. Since the National Guard – including the Garde Mobile – was recruited by conscription it is hard to measure the extent of French patriotism, but the armies created by the republic could not have existed without substantial popular support. The political revolutionaries and idealists among the leaders of the French war effort took essentially the same view as the generals on both sides: that patriotism, determination and faith could overcome any obstacles to produce victory. But they had much less idea of how large those obstacles were.

As representatives of the German nation in arms, the victorious soldiers were typically peasants or industrial workers, young men far from home in a strange land, hungry and exhausted from marching, brutalised by the experience of battle; and often arrogant as conquerors. Particularly if from southern Germany, they expected to find the provinces of north-east France full of grateful Germans like themselves, and were baffled by the difficult dialect of Alsace and the attitudes that accompanied it. The Bavarian troops at Bazeilles, who claimed to have fought an honest fight against a deceitful and murderous enemy, including the civilians they killed, were reacting to deep cultural differences as well as the heat of the moment. Some soldiers in their writings described this as a racial war.

One consequence of the Franco-Prussian War was a great effort afterwards to codify and clarify the laws of war on what constituted a soldier or a uniform, and on the rights of civilians and prisoners of war.

'The Siege of Strasbourg'. German lithograph. (Ann Ronan Picture Library)

The 1856 Paris Declaration had laid down laws for naval warfare including the banning of privateering by merchant ships. The Franco-Austrian War led directly to the first 'Geneva Convention for the amelioration of the condition of the wounded in armies in the field' in 1864, followed by the first International Conference of the Red Cross in Geneva in 1867, and a further conference in Berlin in 1869. This was the first war between two countries that were signatories to these agreements. The 1868 St Petersburg Declaration, aimed at limiting suffering in warfare, stipulated that 'The only legitimate

Strasbourg cathedral and nearby houses during the Prussian bombardment of the city. Woodcut from *The Graphic*, 15 October 1870. (Ann Ronan Picture Library)

The siege of Paris

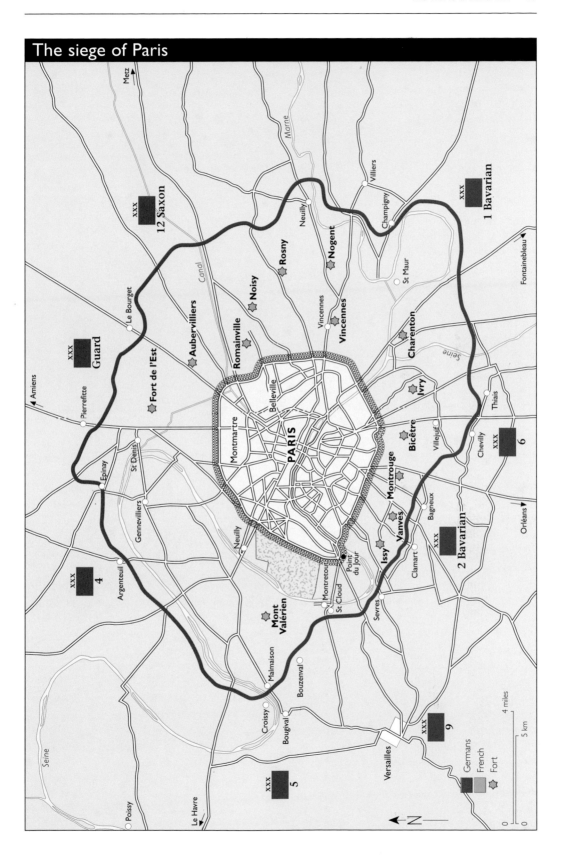

A Prussian siege artilley battery in action. Lithograph.
(Ann Ronan Picture Library)

object which States endeavour to accomplish
during war is to weaken the military forces
of the enemy', part of the growing
distinction between combatants and
non-combatants. After the war, the Brussels
Declaration of 1874 tried to establish
international law for the conduct of
occupying armies, including that those
civilians who 'on the approach of the enemy,
spontaneously take up arms to resist the
invading troops' should be treated as soldiers
'if they respect the laws and customs of war',
which was not universally accepted.

Just as the new mass armies and weapons
technology had changed battles, so they also
changed the way that sieges were conducted.
Civilian populations had always suffered
alongside soldiers from starvation, disease
and enemy bombardment and assault. But
fortress towns were now defended by a ring
of outlying forts mounting artillery, with the
intention of holding the enemy artillery

back beyond range of the centre. Increases in
artillery ranges could quickly render these
forts useless. The Red Cross sent observers to
the siege of Strasbourg, where the greater
range and accuracy of their new siege
artillery allowed the Prussians the
innovation of deliberately shelling
undefended civilian areas heavily to shock
the city into surrender. Famous buildings
including the city library were destroyed,
and the cathedral damaged. The bishop and
civic leaders pleaded with both Prussian and
French generals for a ceasefire. The
combination of these terror tactics with a
conventional siege led to Strasbourg's
surrender on 28 September, freeing the
Prussian siege-train for use against Paris
and elsewhere. Sieges of fortified towns
occupied many Prussian troops for the
remaining months of the war; Verdun fell
on 8 November.

Apart from their desire to end the war on
their own terms rather than to expand it,
despite the unprecedented size of their forces
the Prussians did not have the troops to

occupy much more of France. Their broad strategy was to maintain the siege of Paris, to protect and improve their own communications across northern France by besieging or capturing French towns along the route, and to hold back any French forces that tried to interfere, on a line roughly from Sedan to Amiens in the north, and from Dijon to Orléans in the south.

The French could have continued a simple guerrilla strategy of harassment with their *franc-tireurs*, or launched a major attack in the east against the long Prussian lines of communication. But an important part of the idea of France for which they were fighting was Paris, not only as a military objective but as a national and cultural symbol. The result was several poorly organised French offensives towards Paris from the south and the north, with political pressure and ideological zeal – and increasingly the fear of a Red revolution in the capital – pushing their forces forward, while lack of training and organisation held them back.

Toul and Strasbourg had fallen by bombardment, but at Metz and Paris the Prussians largely settled down with a ring of troops around the outlying forts and waited. Around Paris, in order to feed their forces the Prussians diverted thousands of troops to appropriating the autumn harvest, reverting to what was for many their civilian occupation as peasant farmers, but in uniform.

Inside Paris itself, a few large balloons were found capable of carrying a man, some of them left over from the 1867 Great Exhibition. On 23 September the first was released to float over the Prussian lines to safety, more were built, and fragile communications were established with the outside world. Although General Trochu and other members of the government remained in Paris, on 8 October interior minister Léon

Léon Gambetta (centre, with hat) about to escape from Paris for Tours by balloon on 7 October 1870. French chromolithograph, 1890. (Ann Ronan Picture Library)

A balloon prepares for take-off at night close to the Gare du Nord in central Paris, including passengers, mail, and (in the foreground) carrier pigeons. A contemporary woodcut published in London. (Ann Ronan Picture Library)

Gambetta made this dangerous balloon trip in order to reach Tours, where he also took over the role of minister for war and effective leader of the war effort. Although balloons had been used before in warfare, this was the first war in which military air transport was a significant issue, including the legal argument from the Prussians that a captured balloonist could be shot as a spy.

On 12 October Gambetta announced from Tours the mobilisation of the entire National Guard, and two days later the creation of an 'Auxiliary Army' structure including all Garde Mobile, National Guard and *franc-tireur* forces, to supplement the existing French Army. On 2 November an edict was issued which in theory conscripted every able-bodied Frenchman of 21–40 years old. Nearly 700,000 men and 36 divisions were raised to fight before the end of January 1871. What was lacking was the time for proper training before they were pushed into battle. Officers were dismissed from the Army, and others appointed to the Auxiliary Army, for political reasons rather than military competence. Commanders of armies changed frequently, and command was often disputed or shared; army corps were usually well below strength and composed of a mixture of troops; and although French artillery was improving, trained and experienced gunners were in short supply. Enthusiasm and patriotism might be quite real, but they were not enough by themselves to withstand the stress of battle.

Within Metz, about 180,000 French troops were trapped together with a civilian population of about 70,000, with no adequate provision having been made for food. From 4 September onwards the French fell back on the traditional expedient of eating their horses. Several attacks were made against the Prussian lines with the capture of harvested grain as the main objective. French soldiers trying to desert or surrender, and civilians escaping the siege, were turned back by the Prussians. On 14 October Metz introduced bread rationing for civilians, but otherwise the amount of food obtained was regulated entirely to the cost, which increased dramatically. Both the ethics and the practicalities of the treatment of what military men called the 'useless mouths' of civilians in a siege became a major issue of the war. As the autumn

Prussian troops enter Metz after the French surrender. Woodcut from the *Illustrated London News*, 12 November 1870. This illustration also gives a good idea of the problems the French encountered moving their own troops through the centre of Metz before the battles of Mars-la-Tour and Gravellotte-St Privat in August. (Ann Ronan Picture Library)

weather worsened, Metz began to suffer from the lethal epidemic diseases that accompanied all long sieges, the product of poor diet, poor sanitation and overcrowding: bronchitis, dysentery and cholera at first, then typhus and smallpox. Despite the efficient Prussian military medical service, the besieging troops also fell victims to the same diseases. On 27 October Bazaine and the Army of Metz surrendered into captivity. This not only released the besieging Prussian

'The Surrender of Metz to Crown Prince Frederick
Charles.' Woodcut by Conrad Freyberg (born 1842)
showing the formal surrender of Bazaine's forces.
(Ann Ronan Picture Library)

troops for other uses, it was also another
terrible shock throughout France.

As one of the great cities of the world,
Paris was a contrast between its wealth and
glitter, and the extreme poverty of some of its
working-class districts. The wide boulevards
built under Napoleon III had cleared away
some of the worst slums, and also served a
military purpose: providing clear fields of fire
for troops against any revolutionary mob.
The city was divided into 20 *arrondisements*
(districts), each with its own mayor and local
politics. The Paris National Guard were
recruited by district and allowed to elect their
officers; some working-class battalions elected
radical demagogues and professional
revolutionaries who had spent many years in

prison. Public subscriptions were also
encouraged to symbolically 'buy' cannon for
the National Guard, and many people
considered both the troops and the guns to
belong to them rather than to the French
Army or the government.

At the start of the siege, Trochu estimated
that Paris had food to last for 80 days, or
until mid-November. As the autumn set in,
boredom was soon replaced by rumours and
political protests. With the government
apparently doing nothing, minor attacks
mounted on the Prussian lines were
exaggerated into great victories. The largest of
these came on 27 October when the small
Prussian garrison at Le Bourget village north-
east of the city was overwhelmed. While this
was being celebrated the Prussians counter-
attacked on 30 October and retook the village
with 1,200 French casualties. Together with
the fall of Metz and rumours of a capitulation
to Prussian demands, this produced a political

crisis on 'Black Monday', 31 October, as radical National Guard troops seized Trochu and his government at the *Hôtel de Ville* (city hall), threatening to re-establish the Paris Commune of 1792–94. Negotiations and the deployment of troops loyal to the government produced first a compromise, and next day the arrest of many of the insurgents.

South of Paris, troops led by General Ludwig Frieherr von der Tann-Rathsamhausen, including his own I Bavarian Corps, captured Orléans on 10 October. This autumn fighting in the Loire valley was very different from the battles of August. Marching conditions in the cold and wet through the mud and forests were miserable, and *franc-tireur* attacks were frequent. Formations on both sides were widely dispersed and had even greater difficulty in locating each other. The Prussian Army continued to show its superior organisation and discipline by out-marching

the French, and rarely had difficulty defeating the raw troops sent to attack it. But battles were often haphazard affairs that might last several days, sometimes without a decisive result.

After about a month, the French Army of the Loire concentrated 70,000 troops of XV and XVI Corps in an advance on Orléans. With fewer than 20,000 soldiers, General von der Tann pulled back from the town and gave battle at the village of Coulmiers to the north on 9 November. The result of such a difference in numbers was a French victory enabling them to liberate Orléans, while their enemies pulled back relatively unscathed further north.

The battle of Coulmiers was the first French victory since Saarbrücken on 2 August and the first of any consequence in the war, giving rise to a myth on both sides. The French belief, which was short lived, was that the forces of the Third Republic were a

'Attack of the 2 Rhine Hussar Regiment at Hébécourt, November 1870'. Painting c.1880 by Emil Huenten (1827–1902) depicting one of the numerous actions in the later part of the war. (AKG, Berlin)

match for the Prussian Army. The Prussian belief, which long outlasted the war, was that the Bavarians were inferior soldiers. Shortly afterwards, command of the reinforced Prussian and Bavarian troops, designated a 'detachment' rather than an army, was given to Frederick-Francis Grand Duke of Mecklenburg-Schwerin, formerly commanding the Prussian XIII Corps.

During November the progressive arrival of the forces of Prince Frederick Charles' Second Army released by the fall of Metz brought the Prussian forces facing Orléans to over 100,000 troops, including cavalry, spread out over a wide area. A renewed clash between troops of Second Army and the Army of the Loire took place north of Orléans on 28 November at the battle of Beaune (from the nearest location, Beaune-le-Rolande), when a French attack was repulsed. The autumn rain now turned

to winter frost and snow. To co-operate with an attempt by the forces from Paris to break through the Prussian encirclement in what was called the 'Great Sortie', the Army of the Loire attacked again on 1–2 December in the battle of Loigny (or Second Battle of Orléans). This was a major Prussian victory, leading to the recapture of Orléans by 3 December, and to a further victory south-west of the city at Beaugency, in a four-day battle that began on 8 December. On 11 December the French government at Tours relocated to the safety of Bordeaux, far to the south.

Despite the winter conditions the Prussians continued to drive the Army of the Loire back, splitting the French forces in two and then leaving the broken halves to retreat in different directions, south to Bourges and west to Le Mans. As they did so, in the appalling weather the French suffered from desertions, sickness and surrenders, part of their forces reaching Le Mans on 19 December in a state of collapse. Other than the lack of any pressing military need, the Prussians did not pursue the Army of the

Loire partly because the strain of a long campaign in such conditions was causing even their discipline to break down. By mid-December, I Bavarian Corps, which had been involved the longest, was close to useless from illness and exhaustion, and other units were deteriorating at the same rate. After allowing its troops to recover, the Prussian Second Army attacked westwards on 4 January 1871, again in frost and snow, against what was now designated the First Army of the Loire. This culminated in another major Prussian victory at the battle of Le Mans on 7–12 January, which captured the town and effectively ended the fighting south of Paris.

The campaigns elsewhere followed a similar pattern on a smaller scale. After the surrender of Metz, the Prussian First Army, now commanded by General Edwin von

'The Hessians at Chambord, 9 December 1870'. After a watercolour c.1900 by Richard Knoetel (1857–1914), depicting another action in the war. (AKG, Berlin)

Manteuffel, was sent to defend against a developing threat from the French Army of the North, of about 17,000 men. The first major clash came at the battle of Amiens (or Villers-Bretonneux) on 27 November, a Prussian victory leading to their capture of the city as the French fell back northwards to Arras. Manteuffel's forces continued to advance westward, capturing Rouen on 5 December. Again, both sides suffered from the winter weather, with the poorly equipped French being most affected. In another clash east of Amiens on 23 December, in the battle of Pont-Noyelles (or La Hallue), the Army of the North, now more than 30,000 strong, did rather better in holding most of its positions, but again withdrew northwards to Arras afterwards. The French achieved a minor victory at the battle of Bapaume on 3 January, but the Army of the North once again withdrew to Arras, driven by its own supply problems and the winter conditions. A last attempt by the French to attack and draw off enemy forces

from the siege of Paris ended at the battle of St Quentin (east of Amiens) on 19 January, another hard-fought French defeat which effectively brought the campaign to an end.

The fighting to the east, between Dijon and Belfort, was too distant from Paris to affect the siege directly, but did draw off some Prussian troops and threatened their lines of communication and supply. After the fall of Strasbourg, the Prussian XIV Corps had pushed southwards, and after its first encounters with Garibaldi's troops had laid siege to Belfort, and captured Dijon on 31 October. In one last French effort, after the Army of the Loire was split following the battle of Beaugency, the forces that had reached Bourges – designated the Second Army of the Loire – were sent eastwards by rail to reinforce the troops already fighting near Dijon and to raise the siege of Belfort. Including the French forces already in the east, the Second Army of the Loire numbered about 150,000 under General Bourbaki, the controversial former

commander of the Imperial Guard at Gravelotte-St Privat, who had already been replaced commanding the Army of the North and who was at least partly responsible for the failures around Orléans.

Campaigning in the deep winter of December and January in the mountains close to the Swiss frontier, both sides suffered greater losses from these conditions than from the enemy. In response to the French advance the Prussians pulled back, abandoning Dijon in late December,

followed by a small French success at Villersexel on 9 January. Reinforcements under General von Manteuffel were rapidly sent to the region to form the new Prussian Fifth Army – known as the Army of the South – of about 120,000 troops.

A French popular print rather unrealistically depicting General Bourbaki at the head of his troops at the battle of Villersexel, south-west of Belfort, on 15 January 1871. The troops in the foreground are French Zouaves. (AKG, Berlin)

Troops of Bourbaki's defeated army on their way into internment in Switzerland, 1 February 1871. From a wood engraving. (Ann Ronan Picture Library)

At the battle of Héricourt (or Lisaine) on 15–17 January, Bourbaki's forces failed to break through the short distance north to Belfort, and began their own retreat. In a series of manoeuvres made all the more remarkable by the terrain and the weather, the Prussians then conducted their last encirclement of the war, cutting off the French retreat westward and pinning them against the Swiss frontier. On 26 January Bourbaki, believing that all was hopeless, ordered his soldiers to take refuge in Switzerland, and next day shot himself in the head. By 1 February 85,000 French troops had crossed over the frontier into internment.

Remarkably, Bourbaki's suicide attempt failed and he later recovered from his head wound.

These three campaigns were all intended to help Paris, where by November the Prussian siege had entered a critical phase, as neutral observers noticed a marked increase in gloom. In late November, the French planned the Great Sortie, their major attack on the Prussian lines in order to break the siege. Originally intended to be launched north-westward towards Rouen, this was changed after the false hope of the victory at Coulmiers to an attack south-easterly to co-operate with an advance by the Army of the Loire. The attack by 80,000 men under General Auguste Ducrot was begun on 28 November across the River Marne towards Villers and Champigny, but was held by the Prussians after heavy fighting; the French withdrew back across the Marne on 3 December, having suffered 12,000 casualties. Since the Army of the Loire was defeated at Loigny, not even a successful breakthrough could have helped the French, but the disappointment was considerable.

Paris was now faced with starvation which rationing could no longer help, and turned to any source of food available. A taste for horsemeat, only recently introduced as cheap food for the poor, became well established. Dogs, rats and cats were all eaten. Animals in the zoos, which could not themselves be fed, were shot and cooked; famous restaurants served elephant, tiger and giraffe meat for those who could afford it. By Christmas the siege had lasted almost 100 days. The distinction between the rich, with their own supplies of food, and the rest of Paris was becoming all too apparent. Malnutrition and stress produced 'siege fever', described by one victim 'as if all the centipedes in the world were walking across my brain'. A further attack was mounted against the northern sector of the Prussian encirclement on 21–22 December, with little objective than to show fight. Trochu advised the government at Bordeaux that Paris would exhaust all its food supplies by 20 January.

At Versailles, the Prussian Royal Headquarters was increasingly a centre of politics and intrigue; relations between Bismarck and Moltke, always tense, had

A contemporary French cartoon of the siege of Paris. In the butcher's window are a dog's head ('free from rabies'), a stuffed horse's hoof, and a rat. The sailor, a member of the Paris garrison, is saying 'I can accept dogfish, Madame, but dog!...' (Ann Ronan Picture Library)

become almost unworkable with threats of resignation on both sides. International attitudes, which had generally favoured Prussia, began to move in France's direction as the siege of Paris continued. 'The public opinion of Europe has not remained unaffected by the spectacle', Crown Prince Frederick William of Prussia wrote on 31 December. 'We are no longer looked upon as the innocent sufferers of wrong, but rather as the arrogant victors.' In December the Russian Empire, exploiting French helplessness, renounced part of the 1856 Treaty of Paris that had ended the Crimean War. In response, the British threatened to declare war again on Russia, and the direct involvement of other countries in the Franco-Prussian War seemed imminent. Although the problems of the French were far greater, the Prussian Army also was suffering from the cold and diseases of the siege and of the winter campaigns; drunkenness and the

A butcher's shop in the Boulevard Haussmann (named after the city planner) in central Paris during the siege, showing meat from zoo animals including elephant, ostrich and antelope for sale. From a contemporary wood engraving. (Ann Ronan Picture Library)

breakdown of discipline were becoming concerns. Moltke noted that I Bavarian Corps, which had been rested and brought north to take part in the siege, was 'restored to a strength of 17,500 men', a little over half its number on mobilisation. The war that should have ended in September had to be ended quickly.

On 5 January 98 Prussian heavy guns opened fire on the forts at Issy, Vanves and Montrouge, the preliminary to moving the guns within range of the centre of Paris and ending the siege by bombardment. There had been some shelling already, but this was a deliberate attempt to frighten Paris into surrender, killing civilians including children indiscriminately. The large Salpetrière Hospital was frequently hit, despite the new symbol of the Red Cross on its roof, marking the start of many subsequent arguments about intent or accident. Another argument to emerge from the bombardment was that far from frightening the population of Paris, it only

made them more determined. Over three weeks, 12,000 shells were fired into the city, damaging 1,400 buildings, but causing only 375 casualties including 97 dead. But the deep cold – enough to freeze the River Seine – and the shortages of food and fuel for warmth continued. Deaths from disease escalated, with almost 4,500 being recorded in the final week. Calls for a change of government, and for a revolutionary Commune, became more widespread. On 19 January an attack by the National Guard was made to the west aimed at Buzenval, but was also defeated, a few days after the Prussian capture of Le Mans.

His position now impossible, General Trochu was replaced as military governor of Paris by General Joseph Vinoy. 'My presence was no longer useful,' he observed, with an echo of Napoleon III at Châlons. Trochu remained notionally president of the republic, a function that in reality Léon Gambetta was carrying out at Bordeaux. On 22 January revolutionary National Guards again fired upon government buildings in the centre of Paris, including the Hôtel de Ville. At midnight on 27 January, after Jules Favre had agreed to Bismarck's terms, an armistice ending the war came into force.

Mr Archibald Forbes

Just as with soldiers, so with civilians in the war – it was the famous and the educated who have left the most accessible records. In French village communities and in the slums of Paris, levels of education and literacy rarely rose above the basic. The views of several famous French literary figures about the war have survived. Gustave Flaubert wrote on its outbreak: 'I am mortified with disgust at the stupidity of my countrymen.' On the collapse of the Second Empire, George Sand (Amadine Dupin) exalted that 'This is the third awakening; and it is beautiful beyond imagination. Hail to you, Republic!' The establishment of the republic also prompted 68-year-old Victor Hugo to return from 15 years in exile to resume his political life, playing a prominent part in Paris during the siege with the National Guard. 'Paris is the city of cities,' he proclaimed publicly. 'There has been an Athens, there has been a Rome, and there is a Paris.'

During the siege of Paris and the Commune, all citizens – including numerous seasonal migrant workers from other parts of France, in professions varying from building to prostitution – found themselves caught up in the fighting. A prominent part was played by Georges Clemenceau, the young radical Mayor of Montmartre, whose efforts to reconcile the Communards and the government ended in failure but who later became famous as premier of France from 1917 to 1918. The poet Paul Verlaine worked in the Communard press office, while the painter Auguste Renoir only narrowly escaped being lynched as a spy. As in other wars, the proper role of women was a matter of ideological dispute, and for them to carry arms was itself seen as revolutionary. The veteran anarchist Louise Michel, 'the Red Virgin', organised a women's battalion for the Commune that fought well in Bloody Week, which she survived.

Civilians in Germany were altogether more remote from the war, but mostly even the prominent and educated had no doubt about their own side's superiority and righteousness. The composer Richard Wagner expressed the hope that Paris would be burnt to the ground as 'a symbol of the liberation of the world from all that is bad'. His wife Cosima, looking at illustrations of French soldiers in her newspaper, felt that 'the wretchedness and the degeneracy of the people stares out at me' and that 'in these sensual, besotted faces one sees complete idiocy.' Bismarck's wife Johanna also expressed the hope that Paris would be obliterated, and thought it 'disgusting' that French soldiers should receive medical treatment from the Prussian Army; rather 'They should be left to die.' She also felt that the whole French population should be 'shot and stabbed to death, even the little babies'. This extreme attitude may not have been widespread, as French prisoners of war in Germany appear to have been well treated by the civilian population. But except for small numbers of dissidents on either side, and internationalist revolutionaries who condemned them both, the divisions that found expression in the war clearly existed in both civil societies.

All these people experienced part of the war at first hand; but the only civilians whose personal experiences included all of the critical episodes of the war were the reporters of various nationalities who accompanied the French and Prussian forces. These included the Anglo-Irish William Howard Russell of *The Times* of London, the man who had first earned the title 'war correspondent' for his reporting of the Crimean War. Another British correspondent, whose reports formed the

French North African troops as prisoners of war meeting civilians including children in their prison camp at Wahn near Cologne. The British correspondent who reported on this scene remarked particularly on the improved treatment of prisoners due to the Geneva Convention. Woodcut appearing in *The Graphic*, 22 October 1870. (Ann Ronan Picture Library)

basis for his two-volume memoir of the war, was the Scotsman Archibald Forbes of the London *Morning Advertiser* and *Daily News*. The Franco-Prussian War began a golden age for war correspondents, and Forbes explained why: the direct link by telegraph, and the fact that with longer-range weapons to see a battle meant being placed in great danger, required both a new style of reporting and a remarkable man to do it. His writings illustrate the manner in which newspaper reporters were starting to adopt the role of civilian witnesses to military events for their readers.

Many war reporters have been flamboyant characters, and it is sometimes hard to

separate fact from embellishment in Forbes' writings. Born in Morayshire, Scotland, in 1838, he was remembered as a small, opinionated man with a massive moustache. The son of a clergyman, he attended Aberdeen University but ran into debt and left without qualifications, enlisting as a trooper in the 1st (Royal) Dragoons in 1859, and rising to acting quartermaster-sergeant before being discharged in 1864. He was self-taught in military affairs, writing articles and meeting officers from several countries.

The Franco-Prussian War established Forbes' reputation as a war correspondent. The language barrier does not seem to have been a great problem; Forbes spoke some German and French, and London was the temporary home of a community of Germans who as war threatened patriotically returned to serve in their respective armies. Forbes journeyed out with some of these men, and remembered even two young New York businessmen, a combination of

'Germano-Yankee financial cuteness and pure single-hearted patriotic zeal' who had crossed the Atlantic to fight.

Forbes reached Cologne on 19 July 1870 and was attached to Second Army under Prince Frederick Charles, which he stayed with through to the trapping of Bazaine's forces in Metz. He recorded many human details and tragedies of the war as it affected civilians. A Prussian sergeant was due to be married, and rather than be left behind his future wife had joined him at Saarbrücken; the ceremony was about to start when the French attacked and captured the town. Forbes found the bridegroom after the battle of Spicheren, dead with a bullet through his throat.

Forbes was an eyewitness to the battle of Mars-la-Tour on 16 August, making the comparison between the Death Ride and the Charge of the Light Brigade. He also witnessed the battle of Gravelotte-St Privat, afterwards visiting Gravelotte village church, used as a makeshift surgery. 'The white altar-cloth was splashed with blood, the floor was bedded all over with wounded, and the atmosphere had become tainted and malaria-laden'.

Forbes left the forces surrounding Metz shortly after the siege began and attached himself to the Royal Headquarters, accompanying it through to the battle of Sedan. He wrote that while Napoleon III's entourage had offered the French hotels in which they stayed 'promises to pay when the war should be over', Prussian generals paid their hotel bills as they went, and 'the people made no secret of the fact that they liked the Prussian way of doing business best', perhaps ignoring the fact that he was with the Prussian Army when he was told this. He saw the battle of Sedan and the French surrender from the perspective of I Bavarian Corps, writing that 'Napoleon's one wise act was his displaying the white flag' that afternoon. Forbes then continued on with the Royal Headquarters on the

Prussian officers billeted on a French family, December 1871. A contemporary engraving depicting a scene similar to those witnessed and described by Archibald Forbes. (Ann Ronan Picture Library)

march to Paris and Versailles, before returning to Second Army besieging Metz, getting himself attached to the 4th East Prussian Grenadier Regiment and reporting on the daily experience of the front-line troops. He was critical of the lack of hygiene and poor standards of living in nearby peasant villages: 'Before every door a large and venerable dunghill reeked,' he wrote, 'their ooze percolated everywhere and was indescribably fetid.'

After the surrender of Metz, Forbes went back to London for a few days and then returned to report on the siege of Paris from the Prussian side. He saw Le Bourget village after its recapture by the Prussians, noting once more the bloodstains and the damage inside the church, and that the French prisoners were 'so ravenous with hunger that the men grubbed in the gutter after turnip-tops and bones'. In one of his excursions to the north-west of Paris in search of a story, he helped a peasant woman at the village of Argenteuil who had been injured by a French bullet; she told him that her son was a soldier with the Paris garrison and of her 'fanciful supposition that it might have been the bullet fired by the son which struck the mother'. He also recorded that 'many circumstances occurred during this campaign, tending to imperil the continued existence of the Geneva Convention', which had only recently come into force, and that each side 'had stories of asserted atrocities to narrate against the other'. He celebrated Christmas as the guest of 103rd (4th Royal Saxon) Infantry Regiment, contrasting their meal including caviar and fresh butter with conditions inside Paris.

On entering Paris after the siege, Forbes found it 'haunted by the peculiar half-sweetish, half-fetid odour which horse-flesh gives out in cooking', and was concerned in case his own riding horse was taken from him. He witnessed the German parade through Paris on 1 March 1871, and had to be rescued by sympathetic National Guards, after being attacked by the crowd for showing too much politeness to the troops and replying to a question in German. He reported also 'a woman whom the Paris mob had stripped and painted diverse colours, because she had been caught parlaying with a Prussian drummer', and was able to help two aristocratic ladies who were starving, but would not take the free food being distributed, because they were too proud to accept charity.

Having accompanied Kaiser Wilhelm back to Berlin, Forbes then returned to London to start work on his account of the war, but came back out to report on the Commune. In the centre of Paris an old lady surprised him by calmly identifying the sounds of the various guns, distinguishing incoming and outgoing shellfire. In the assault by MacMahon's troops, a bullet went through his hat and he was nearly shot as a Communard, but was able to travel to London and back during Bloody Week to file his stories on the events.

The last words in Forbes' account of the war are on the return to Berlin of the 2nd Guard Landwehr Regiment, which had seen some hard fighting. These were mostly men with families, who a few months earlier would never have expected to fight a war. After marching past Kaiser Wilhelm, they were dismissed back to civilian life. 'The men were free to kiss wives, hug bairns [children], and shake hands with friends. Surely no better finis can I find for my book,' Forbes wrote.

Forbes continued his career after 1871, reporting on the Carlist War in Spain of 1872–76, the Serbian War of 1876, the Russo-Turkish War of 1877–78, the Second Afghan War of 1878–80 and the Zulu War of 1879, becoming famous for his own exploits on campaign, and for his increasingly critical style of writing, not hesitating to condemn generals. For carrying dispatches during the Zulu War his newspaper, the *Illustrated London News*, demanded that he should be given the Victoria Cross, although civilians were not eligible for any medals. After this, Forbes' declining health ended his war reporting, but he continued writing and lecturing on military matters in Britain. He died in 1900, in a fevered delirium in the arms of his editor, was buried in Aberdeen, and has a memorial crypt in St Paul's Cathedral, London.

The Paris Commune

For the last month of the war, the French had been fighting against what was officially a new enemy. Starting from political negotiations between Prussia and its allies in October, the German Empire was proclaimed on 1 January 1871. The participation of the south German states in the war meant their inevitable inclusion with Prussia and the North German Confederation in the 'little Germany' version of the empire, which was in constitutional terms an agglomeration of 26 states, each with its own particular form of government and institutions. King Wilhelm I disliked the idea at first, and both he and Bismarck, who became chancellor of the empire, saw it chiefly as an extension of Prussia, their first loyalty.

The symbolism of the German Empire's creation, in a series of public and private ceremonies over three months, at each stage humiliated France and emphasised its replacement by Germany as the dominant power in Europe. This began on 18 January 1871, when King Wilhelm was proclaimed Emperor, or *Kaiser* Wilhelm I of Germany at a ceremony in the Hall of Mirrors at Versailles, the palace of the French kings and of Napoleon I.

The terms of the armistice were an immediate ceasefire in Paris from 28 January, extending to the rest of France by 31 January. All French Army troops except for one division must lay down their arms, but not the Paris National Guard, since Favre judged it politically impossible to disarm them.

Kaiser Wilhelm I of Germany being proclaimed in the Hall of Mirrors at Versailles on 18 January 1871. The religious as well as political symbolism of this ceremony is apparent. From a wood engraving. (Ann Ronan Picture Library)

The armistice would continue until 19 February while elections took place for a new French government that would agree lasting peace terms. If no peace had been agreed, then either side could resume fighting. Favre obtained from Bismarck the concession that the French guns could fire the last shot of the Paris siege, and that no Prussian troops would enter Paris during the armistice. In Bordeaux, Gambetta resigned, both in protest and to clear the way for the new government.

The French elections took place on 8 February, and the National Assembly convened at Bordeaux. In the traditional pattern of French voting, a majority of the 768 seats went to Monarchists, political Catholics and other Conservatives; only about

150 of the deputies were Republicans and fewer than 20, including Gambetta, were Radicals. Victor Hugo and Georges Clemenceau were among the 43 deputies elected by Paris; Garibaldi was also elected as a deputy, but resigned soon afterwards. The political message was clear: the Third Republic could perhaps stay, but France wanted peace even at the German price. The assembly adopted as its leader the 73-year-old Adolphe Thiers, a veteran conservative politician who had last held office under King Louis-Philippe in the July Monarchy, and who had been heavily involved in the peace negotiations.

On 26 February at Versailles, Thiers signed the preliminary peace terms. These were, like so much about the Franco-Prussian War, a

mixture of the traditional and the modern. France gave up Alsace including Strasbourg, and the northern part of Lorraine including Metz. It was to pay Germany an indemnity of 5,000 million francs (equivalent at the time to £200 million or US$1,000 million – the average wage of a Paris worker was less than five francs a day) including 200 million francs from Paris itself. Of this, Germany would receive 1,000 million francs within 12 months and the balance within three years, continuing to occupy eastern France including Belfort with 50,000 troops as a guarantee of payment, but withdrawing this garrison progressively once 2,000 million francs were paid. Bismarck made no demands about France's colonial empire, nor

were any long-term limitations imposed on the size and nature of the French Army and Navy. Until the national assembly confirmed these terms, the German Army would station 30,000 men in Paris. If there was no agreement by 3 March, either side could resume fighting at three day's notice.

On 1 March the National Assembly voted 546 to 107 (with 23 abstentions) to accept the preliminary peace of Versailles. Gambetta resigned again, as did Victor Hugo, other deputies from Paris and of course the deputies from Alsace and Lorraine. On the same day, 30,000 troops of the German Army paraded in triumph before Kaiser Wilhelm and then past the Arc de Triomphe (their leading cavalry rode through the great arch despite obstacles placed there) and through the centre of Paris. Only the rapid arrival of Jules Favre with news that the peace had been agreed prevented further parades on the following days; and on 3 March the Germans withdrew their troops.

The National Assembly followed this by passing a number of conservative measures that seemed aimed at enraging working-class Paris, including laws requiring all debts incurred in the war to be paid at once, especially rents; ending the daily wage paid to the National Guard; and appointing as its new commander General Claude d'Aurelle de Paladines, a reactionary former Bonapartist. Leading members of the revolt against Trochu in Paris on 'Black Monday' back on 31 October, including the radical Auguste Blanqui, were sentenced to death. The assembly then dissolved itself on 10 March, to reconvene at Versailles – not in Paris itself – 10 days later.

The new Kaiser Wilhelm returned to Berlin in triumph along with the first troops of his new German Army, and marching processions were held through the city streets. On 21 March the new assembly of the German Empire, the *Reichstag*, met in

'Fighting at Villejuif, 19 September 1870.' A painting by Eduard Detaille (1848–1912) depicting Paris cannon in action at the village of Villejuif on the southern side of the defences. (Ann Ronan Picture Library)

Berlin. The only opposition to the terms of the peace including the annexation of Alsace and Lorraine came from the small Social Democratic Party. The German Empire took as its national day 2 September, the day of the French surrender at Sedan.

With the armistice, the remaining troops of the German Army stayed encircling Paris, but people were allowed through their lines, and emergency rations were delivered to the starving city. Other relief supplies arrived in early February, chiefly as gifts from Great Britain and the United States. As contact with the outside world was re-established, many middle-class Parisians left the capital, further strengthening radical domination of the National Guard, and demonstrations began against the peace terms and the planned German parade. On 26 February 1871 National Guard troops appropriated 200 cannon that had been bought by subscription during the siege, taking them to the radical stronghold of Montmartre, and forming a central committee of radicals and revolutionaries.

With the French Army effectively disarmed by the Germans, this made the Paris National Guard the strongest military force that France possessed. On 18 March a contingent from the French Army in Paris, about 15,000 men, was ordered up to Montmartre to recover the cannon. In a confused episode the troops refused to obey orders; an excited mob seized their commander, General Claude-Martin Lecomte, together with General Clément Thomas, the National Guard's former commander, and both were shot. Remaining members of the National Government and loyal troops fled or withdrew from Paris. A red flag was flown from the Hôtel de Ville, proclaiming the revolution.

Their own success caught the revolutionaries by surprise; their first acts were to legislate changes in the local government of Paris, including debts and rents, and they continued to issue proclamations in the name of the republic. On 26 March a city-wide election confirmed them in office, and two days later at the Hôtel de Ville they announced themselves as the Commune of

Paris (literally, a 'community' or town council), invoking the revolutionary spirit of 1792–94 but also promising greater self-government for the city.

The creation of the Commune had as much to do with ideology and symbolism as with any political programme, and its members spent much time debating among themselves what they represented; although few were genuinely working class, they included social reformers as well as anarchists, and also one or two prominent women. Although smaller uprisings took place in other French cities, notably Marseilles, this was once again almost entirely a Paris phenomenon, gaining no national support. Even Garibaldi condemned it, returning to Italy, while Victor Hugo sought exile in Brussels.

While the Commune debated its own meaning, the new French government was thoroughly alarmed. Although prepared to negotiate with Bismarck, Thiers took a very different view of the Communards, intending to recapture Paris when his forces were strong enough. Under the Versailles agreement, the Germans gave up control of the territory south of the Seine to the French Army. On Palm Sunday, 2 April, French Army troops – called *Versaillais* by the Communards – mounted an attack from the east near Neuilly, close to the sector from which the Great Sortie had been launched in October. Next day a Communard force – described as resembling 'a hoard of turbulent picnickers' – that set out to attack the National Assembly at Versailles itself was fired upon by artillery from the fort at Mont Valérien, and mostly fled.

The original idealism of the Commune rapidly shrank into mutual accusations, with a decree that hostages would be taken and executed if necessary. This was followed, as with the original Commune of 1792–94, with the resignation, flight or arrest of moderates, the creation of a 'Committee of Public Safety', and a progressive descent into dictatorship by terror. A shorter second siege and bombardment of Paris began, with the Versailles forces firing into the city, and minor probing attacks from both sides.

Fighting between loyal French troops and Communard National Guardsmen in the Pére Lachaise Cemetery in the centre of Paris during the suppression of the Commune. A wood engraving by Albert Robida (1848–1926) from the Paris newspaper *Le Monde Illustré*, 24 June 1871. (Ann Ronan Picture Library)

The German government was as hostile to the idea of the Commune as the French, and Bismarck agreed to changes in their peace agreement, first allowing 80,000 French troops to be sent north of the Loire, and then the rapid release of prisoners of war from Germany to rebuild the French Army. Otherwise, the German response to the Commune was to maintain their own positions and to prevent any movement into Paris through their lines. On 6 April Marshal MacMahon, who had returned from captivity in Germany, replaced General Vinoy as military governor with the responsibility of recapturing Paris. Within the city barricades were built and defences organised; but by the end of the month the Commune forces numbered no more than 30,000 effective troops, and critical strongpoints were being abandoned or left undefended.

The doomed Commune took refuge in symbolism and legend. The Committee of Public Safety started dating its decrees by the old calendar of the original 1789 Revolution. On 15 May, Thiers' own house in Paris was destroyed by decree; and next day the massive Vendôme Column, erected by Napoleon I to celebrate his victories in 1805, was ceremonially toppled as a symbol of imperialism and militarism. There were even plans to obliterate Notre Dame Cathedral. The shelling from the Versailles troops continued, mostly directed at the south-west corner of the Paris defences, including the forts at Issy and Vanves, and the nearby Point-du-Jour Gate. Finally, on the evening of Sunday 21 May, the Point-du-Jour Gate was discovered to have been abandoned and left undefended, and MacMahon's troops entered Paris.

The next seven days became known in France as 'Bloody Week'. As 70,000 troops advanced into the city, greeted by some Parisians as liberators, the Commune issued its last call to the barricades that had been built across the boulevards and through the city centre. Fighting was fierce and confused: 'They shot you first and apologised to your corpse afterwards', wrote one survivor. But by Tuesday the red flag had been hauled down and replaced by the French tricolour, and street battles gave way to executions by firing squads. Fires broke out in many prominent buildings, some of them ordered deliberately by the Communards, and only extinguished by the rain that began on Friday. Among the Commune's last acts were the executions of some of those taken hostage or imprisoned, including the Archbishop of Paris, Monseigneur Georges Darboy. The final stand of the Communards took place in Belleville on Whit Sunday, 28 May, followed by further executions and imprisonments as the Thiers government obliterated the last of the Paris Commune.

Among these dramatic events the remaining legal formalities took place to finally end the Franco-Prussian War. On 10 May the preliminary peace agreement of Versailles was confirmed by the Treaty of Frankfurt. This was ratified by the French National Assembly at Versailles on 17 May, and copies exchanged between the French and German governments on 21 May, the day on which MacMahon's troops entered Paris. The Germans had lost 28,208 soldiers dead and 88,488 wounded in the war. French military losses are less well documented for understandable reasons, but were estimated at about 150,000 dead and the same number wounded. The losses to the French Army in the suppression of the Commune including Bloody Week were 873 killed. Deaths from disease and destitution in both armies were almost certainly greater than losses caused by the enemy. French civilian deaths, including those in the siege of Paris and other sieges like Strasbourg and Metz, cannot be calculated. Including Bloody Week and the deaths that followed it, civilian losses in the Paris Commune have been estimated at about 25,000 dead.

The indemnity due from France to Germany for the war was paid more quickly than expected. By September 1873 Belfort and all temporarily occupied territory had been returned and the last German soldiers had left French soil, except for the territories of Alsace and Lorraine, which were now part of the German Empire.

The war in history

The Franco-Prussian War is seen as a major historical turning point, a moment of departure into a different world. Partly this was due to circumstances that helped shape the war rather than being shaped by it. In the following generation the growing impact of modernity in social, economic and cultural terms transformed much of Europe, as ordinary life became more industrialised and urban, and mass society became even more important. The same period featured considerable increases in emigration from Europe, and the last great expansion of the European colonial empires.

The peace settlement of 1871 is usually described as harsh and the harbinger of inevitable future conflict. Certainly France never forgot or forgave. In the Place de la Concorde in central Paris, where statues symbolise the great cities of France, the figure of Strasbourg was draped in a black shroud of mourning. Emile Zola's novel of the French defeat, *Le Débacle*, appeared in 1892. The French Army talked of *la revanche* – revenge – against Germany. But in fact the Treaty of Frankfurt ushered in the longest period of peace between the Great Powers of Europe for more than 200 years. Other than the Russo-Turkish War of 1877–78, there was no major war involving any of the Great Powers for the rest of the century, and even the Concert of Europe was invoked for the last time at the Congress of Berlin in 1878.

The central political fact of the Franco-Prussian War was the replacement of France by Germany as the dominant power in Europe. France never recovered the position that it held in 1870; after the war the country was slower to continue industrialising than Germany, and fell decisively behind Great Britain as Europe's leading financial power and foreign investor. The struggle between France and Germany

was renewed in the First World War. Although France emerged once more as the stronger power, it was in a Europe that no longer dominated the rest of the world. In the Second World War, just as old people in 1870 had remembered the coming of the Uhlans in 1815, so the German invasion and occupation of France in 1940 evoked the experience of 1870. Sedan was once again a name of ill-omen for the French Army, which suffered a major defeat in 1940 almost on the same battlefields. In 1945 France again emerged victorious in a Europe devastated by war, while the Cold War divided its old enemy into West Germany and East Germany. Reflecting on the disastrous consequences of three wars in a lifetime, French and West German officials determined to tie their countries together by economic and cultural means so tightly that another war between them could never happen. These were the ideological origins of what became the European Union in 1993, following the re-unification of Germany in 1990.

The major personalities of the Franco-Prussian War all faded from the scene soon after 1871. Emperor Napoleon III and his family found safe exile in Great Britain. Seriously ill and heart-broken, Napoleon died in 1873. His son the Prince Imperial – 'Napoleon IV' to Bonapartists – joined the British Army as an artillery officer, and was killed in southern Africa while fighting in the Zulu War of 1879. Empress Eugénie lived until 1920, witnessing the German defeat at the end of the First World War. Adolphe Thiers was confirmed as president of the Third Republic in 1871, but was forced out of office in 1873, and died four years later. Thiers' actions in the war meant that the Third Republic survived as a reasonably stable, capitalist and conservative country at peace with its neighbours, rather than a revolutionary or expansionist threat. General Trochu, the controversial president of the Government of National Defence, sat as an Orléanist deputy in the assembly before retiring in 1872, and died in 1896. Léon Gambetta held various political offices, including briefly that of premier of France in 1881, before dying in an accident the next year. Marshal Bazaine became the French scapegoat for the war. In 1873 he was tried for treason and sentenced to life imprisonment, escaped to exile in Spain soon afterwards, and died in 1888. Marshal

'Dropping the Pilot.' A cartoon by John Tenniel from *Punch*, 29 March 1890, depicting Bismarck as the pilot who has steered the German ship of state out of harbour disembarking, while Kaiser Wilhelm II looks on. (Ann Ronan Picture Library)

MacMahon succeeded Thiers as president of France from 1873 to 1879, dying in 1893.

On the German side, Moltke became Field Marshal Count Helmuth von Moltke, dying in 1891. He is known as 'Moltke the Elder', not from his age but because his nephew Colonel General Helmuth von Moltke also played a significant role in history, as Chief of the German Great General Staff in 1914. Kaiser Wilhelm I died in 1888. His son the Crown Prince became Kaiser Frederick III (the numbering coming from two Holy Roman Emperors called Frederick) for three months before succumbing to cancer, and was succeeded by his son as Kaiser Wilhelm II. The legendary 'Iron Chancellor' Otto von Bismarck, who had been awarded the title of prince after the war, was unable to work with the new Kaiser. He resigned from office in 1890 and died eight years later.

The immediate reaction of the rest of Europe to the defeat of France and the new united Germany was generally favourable. Germany after 1871 was a satisfied power, and France was not by itself strong enough to challenge it again. In 1873 Germany came to agreements with Russia and Austria–Hungary known as the Three Emperors' League (*Dreikaiserbund*) to maintain good relations. In 1879 Germany also formed the Dual Alliance with Austria–Hungary; but although the Three Emperors' League was renewed in 1881 it began to break down under the rivalry between Russia and Austria–Hungary over Slav nationalism in the Balkans. In 1882 Italy joined Germany and Austria–Hungary in the Triple Alliance. In 1890, Bismarck's successors allowed the 1887 Reinsurance Treaty with Russia to lapse, marking the final end of the Three Emperors' League; and in 1894 France and Russia concluded a military alliance, giving France the support it needed against Germany for another war.

Great Britain, despite giving sanctuary to Napoleon III, shared many German attitudes towards the French, and did not regard Germany as hostile, as long as it did not threaten the vast British Empire overseas. As late as 1898, when both Germany and the United States were challenging British economic and industrial pre-eminence, war with France seemed more likely to the British than war with Germany, with Russia as the major threat to British interests outside Europe. It was only in 1904, in the face of growing German ambitions, that the British concluded the *Entente Cordiale* ('friendly understanding') with France that brought them into the First World War in 1914. Just as the French talked of revenge, so the German Army talked increasingly of *Der Tag* – the day – when both France and Great Britain would finally be crushed and Germany would achieve its rightful place.

In two very different responses to the Paris Commune, in 1871 Eugene Pottier wrote the words to the *Internationale*, the anthem of Communist revolutionaries, and the French National Assembly approved the inauguration of the Basilica of Sacré Coeur at Montmartre in atonement for the event. On the day of the war's outbreak, Pope Pius IX at the First Vatican Council announced the doctrine of papal infallibility when speaking *ex cathedra* on faith or morals. This declaration of supreme spiritual power was followed by the withdrawal of the French garrison from Rome because of the Franco-Prussian War, and in September 1870 the city became the capital of Italy. A temporary agreement in 1871 was confirmed by the Lateran Treaty of 1929, when Italy recognised the Vatican City as an independent state.

The Reds and the Paris Commune became identified after 1871 with the Communists and the International, who appropriated the event for themselves. Karl Marx's analysis of the Commune, *The Civil War in France of 1871*, was seen as his most influential work since *The Communist Manifesto*. The successes and failures of the Commune had a major impact on Communist planning of later revolutions, and became an important symbol. When V.I. Lenin died his body was wrapped in a red flag from the Commune, and in 1964 the *Voskhod* Soviet space mission took a ribbon from a Communard

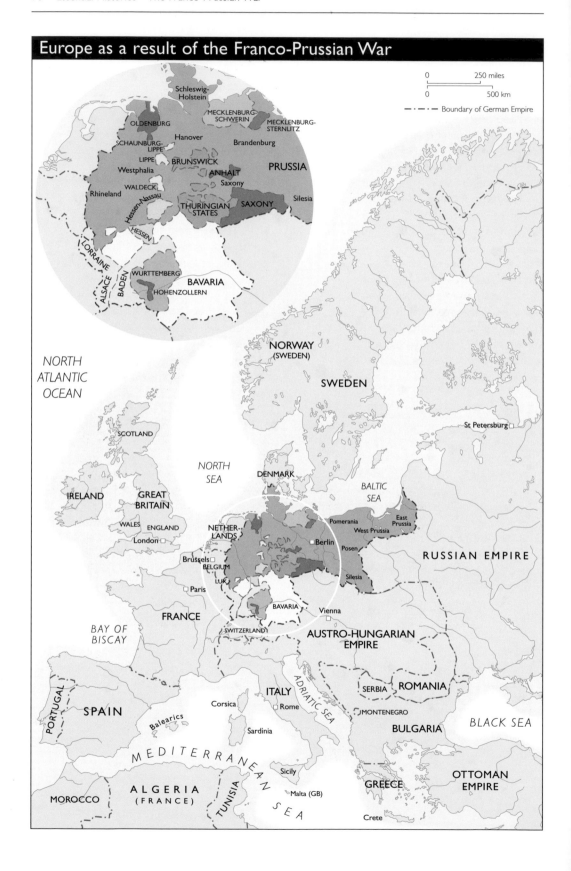

Europe as a result of the Franco-Prussian War

| 0 | | 250 miles |
| 0 | | 500 km |

— · — · — Boundary of German Empire

Schleswig-Holstein

MECKLENBURG-SCHWERIN

MECKLENBURG-STERNLITZ

OLDENBURG

Hanover

Brandenburg

SCHAUNBURG-LIPPE

LIPPE

Westphalia

BRUNSWICK

ANHALT

PRUSSIA

Saxony

Rhineland

WALDECK

Hessen-Nassau

Silesia

THURINGIAN STATES

SAXONY

HESSEN

LORRAINE

ALSACE

BADEN

WURTTEMBERG

HOHENZOLLERN

BAVARIA

NORTH ATLANTIC OCEAN

NORWAY
(SWEDEN)

SWEDEN

St Petersburg ☐

SCOTLAND

NORTH SEA

DENMARK

BALTIC SEA

IRELAND

GREAT BRITAIN

WALES   ENGLAND

London ☐

NETHER-LANDS

Pomerania

West Prussia

East Prussia

☐ Berlin

Posen

Brussels ☐

BELGIUM

LUX

Silesia

RUSSIAN EMPIRE

☐ Paris

BAVARIA

Vienna ☐

FRANCE

SWITZERLAND

AUSTRO-HUNGARIAN EMPIRE

BAY OF BISCAY

ITALY

ADRIATIC SEA

SERBIA

ROMANIA

PORTUGAL

SPAIN

Corsica

☐ Rome

MONTENEGRO

BLACK SEA

Balearics

Sardinia

BULGARIA

M E D I T E R R A N E A N   S E A

Sicily

ALGERIA
(FRANCE)

TUNISIA

Malta (GB)

GREECE

OTTOMAN EMPIRE

MOROCCO

Crete

flag into global orbit together with pictures of Marx and Lenin.

After 1871 German military ideas and culture replaced those of France around the world as the model to be imitated. Young men copied the short German Army haircut, much to the disgust of their elders. Most countries adopted German-style uniforms including the Pickelhaube helmet, the last traces of which remained a century later in the headgear of London policemen. Even emergent Japan in the 1880s employed German instructors to imbue its soldiers with their values. In direct imitation of Germany, by 1914 all European powers had a general staff, all except Great Britain had conscription on the German model, and all had essentially the same philosophy of rapid mobilisation of mass armies at the start of a war, their concentration by railway and a sudden violent invasion of the enemy country.

The Franco-Prussian War was studied after 1871 by military academies and staffs as the model for future war in Europe. In general terms, not very much changed up to 1914. Railways were still the key to large-scale movement; the motor vehicle and the aeroplane were at an early stage of development; and there was still no replacement for the cavalry. Communications also remained much the same; although the telephone and the radio transmitter had been added to the telegraph none of them could function well on a battlefield. But the new generation of weapons that appeared at the end of the 19th century – artillery, rifles and machine guns – were an even bigger leap forward in

'Episode during the Siege of Paris.' Painting by Gustave Doré (1832–83) showing a nun walking through the snow-covered, bloodstained street on an errand of mercy in spite of the bombardment. (Ann Ronan Picture Library)

Index

Visit the Osprey website

- Information about forthcoming books

- Author information

- Read extracts and see sample pages

- Sign up for our free newsletters

- Competitions and prizes

www.ospreypublishing.com